Technically Wrong

ALSO BY SARA WACHTER-BOETTCHER

Content Everywhere

Design for Real Life (with Eric Meyer)

Technically Wrong

Sexist Apps, Biased Algorithms, and Other Threats of Toxic Tech

Sara Wachter-Boettcher

W. W. NORTON & COMPANY
INDEPENDENT PUBLISHERS SINCE 1923
NEW YORK   LONDON

For information about permission to reproduce selections from this book, write to Permissions, W. W. Norton & Company, Inc., 500 Fifth Avenue, New York, NY 10110

For information about special discounts for bulk purchases, please contact W. W. Norton Special Sales at specialsales@wwnorton.com or 800-233-4830

Manufacturing by LSC Communications, Harrisonburg
Book design by Daniel Lagin
Production manager: Anna Oler

Library of Congress Cataloging-in-Publication Data

Names: Wachter-Boettcher, Sara, author.
Title: Technically wrong : sexist apps, biased algorithms, and other threats of
    toxic tech / Sara Wachter-Boettcher.
Description: First edition. | New York, NY : W.W. Norton & Company,
    independent publishers since 1923, [2017] | Includes bibliographical
    references and index.
Identifiers: LCCN 2017031829 | ISBN 9780393634631 (hardcover)
Subjects: LCSH: System failures (Engineering) | Business failures. |
    Technology—Social aspects. | New products—Moral and ethical aspects.
Classification: LCC TA169.5 .W33 2017 | DDC 303.48/34—dc23
LC record available at https://lccn.loc.gov/2017031829

W. W. Norton & Company, Inc.
500 Fifth Avenue, New York, N.Y. 10110
www.wwnorton.com

W. W. Norton & Company Ltd.
15 Carlisle Street, London W1D 3BS

1 2 3 4 5 6 7 8 9 0

For Elena and Audrey, who remind me
that wrongs are always worth righting.

Contents

Chapter 1

Welcome to the Machine

Open your phone's app store or spend a day trawling the tech press, and you'll probably end up a little excited, a little bewildered, and a lot overwhelmed. You can download an app to track your diet, adjust your thermostat, and find a dog walker. You can order dinner—and tip the delivery person—without saying a word or touching your wallet. You can subscribe to weekly meal kits, monthly stylist-selected clothing deliveries, or even quarterly "maker boxes" curated by none other than Bill Nye (yeah, the science guy). The list goes on and on; whatever you want to do, odds are good you can now do it online.

And we are. In late 2015, the Pew Research Center reported that most American adults go online every day, and 20 percent say they're online "almost constantly."[1]

I'm one of them. My days usually start with bouncing between checking the news on Twitter and skimming my inbox for important stuff. While walking to the gym, I'll listen to the news on the NPR One app. While waiting for the train, I'll answer a question from a teammate via Slack, the private-chat-room service. At some point, I'll pop over to Facebook to catch up on babies and cats. In the course of a day, I might make travel plans, check local events, look up historical information, get directions, and do a zillion other things online.

I'm also part of the tech industry. In 2006, I was a twenty-three-year-old aspiring writer from Oregon who had found herself stuck in the Arizona suburbs for a while. I had stumbled my way into a job as a copywriter at a small ad agency. We marketed luxury real estate in planned communities: 5,000-square-foot stucco homes with subzero appliances and infinity-edge pools. Within six months, I'd exhausted all the ways one could possibly describe a house on a golf course in the desert. Then I saw the ad for a web writer. I wasn't sure what a web writer did, to be honest. But I figured, why not? I'd been using the web since AltaVista was the search engine of choice. Besides, whatever the job was, it sounded a hell of a lot more interesting than hawking granite countertops.

It turns out 2007 was a good time to enter tech (and, uh, get as far away from real estate as possible). Facebook was just starting to transform from a college-centric site to the behemoth it's since become. Fledgling messaging service twttr had just renamed itself Twitter. Google had just bought YouTube. The iPhone was about to launch. Pretty soon we'd be watching viral videos, rickrolling our friends, laughing at lolcats—and, of course, managing all that mundane stuff like banking and shopping from our screens. And that meant pretty much every business was aiming not just to have a website, but to figure out how technology might change the way it served its customers.

So here we are, a decade later, and technology is so pervasive

Maslow's hierarchy, updated.

that a version of psychologist Abraham Maslow's hierarchy of needs with "WiFi" added to the base of the pyramid has become one of the most enduring internet memes around.

Even if you're not someone who checks Instagram five times during dinner, you probably rely on connected technology for all kinds of things you used to do in person or over the phone. Applying for a job? Many companies only take applications submitted online. Contacting a business? How would you even find their phone number without visiting their site or asking Google? Booking tickets, researching a candidate, making a restaurant reservation, figuring out bus routes in a new place—sure, you can do all these tasks offline, but it's getting harder to manage it. (Just try to find a good printed map of public transit in the next city you visit.)

As technology shifted, so did my role—morphing from "write something better than 'click here'" to "help us figure out why we have stuff on the web in the first place, and how to communicate there more effectively." I've advised startups, universities, nonprofits, and even massive corporations that are still struggling to move to the web. I've designed large-scale websites, devised publishing strategies, and used many more than my fair share of sticky notes and whiteboards to map out user flows or sketch product features.

Eventually, though, something started to feel off. Despite all the improvements in technology, my peers and I weren't getting better at serving *people*.

It really hit me at the end of 2014, when my friend Eric Meyer—one of the web's early programmers and bloggers—logged onto Facebook. It was Christmas Eve, and he expected the usual holiday photos and well-wishes from friends and families. Instead, Facebook showed him an ad for its new Year In Review feature.

Year In Review allowed Facebook users to create albums of their highlights from the year—top posts, photos from vacations, that sort of thing—and share them with their friends. But Eric wasn't keen on reliving 2014, the year his daughter Rebecca died of aggressive brain cancer. She was six.

Facebook didn't give him a choice. Instead, it created a sample Year In Review album for him, and posted it to his page to encourage him to share it. "Here's what your year looked like!" the copy read. Below it was a picture of Rebecca—the most popular photo Eric had posted all year. And surrounding Rebecca's smiling face and curly hair were illustrations, made by Facebook, of partiers dancing amid balloons and streamers.

Your Year In Review
Eric, here's what your year looked like!
🔒 Only you can see this

See Your Year

The Year In Review promotion that Facebook
created for Eric Meyer. In the center is his daughter
Rebecca, who died of cancer that year. (Eric Meyer)

He was gutted.

"Yes, my year looked like that," he wrote in *Slate* as his story
went viral. "True enough. My year looked like the now-absent
face of my Little Spark. It was still unkind to remind me so tact-
lessly, and without any consent on my part."

Facebook had designed an experience that worked well for
people who'd had a good year, people who had vacations or wed-
dings or parties to remember. But because the design team
focused only on positive experiences, it hadn't thought enough
about what would happen for everyone else—for people whose
years were marred by grief, illness, heartbreak, or disaster.

People like Eric paid the price.

• • •

It's not just Facebook, and it's not just grief or trauma. The more I started paying attention to how tech products are designed, the more I started noticing how often they're full of blind spots, biases, and outright ethical blunders—and how often those oversights can exacerbate unfairness and leave vulnerable people out.

Like in the spring of 2015, when Louise Selby, a pediatrician in Cambridge, England, joined PureGym, a British chain. But every time she tried to swipe her membership card to access the women's locker room, she was denied: the system simply wouldn't authorize her. Finally, PureGym got to the bottom of things: the third-party software it used to manage its membership data—software used at all ninety locations across England—was relying on members' titles to determine which locker room they could access. And the title "Doctor" was coded as male. [2]

Or in March of 2016, when *JAMA Internal Medicine* released a study showing that the artificial intelligence built into smartphones from Apple, Samsung, Google, and Microsoft isn't programmed to help during a crisis. The phones' personal assistants didn't understand words like "rape," or "my husband is hitting me." In fact, instead of doing even a simple web search, Siri—Apple's product—cracked jokes and mocked users. [3]

It wasn't the first time. Back in 2011, if you told Siri you were thinking about shooting yourself, it would give you directions to a gun store. After getting bad press, Apple partnered with the National Suicide Prevention Lifeline to offer users help when they said something that Siri identified as suicidal. But five years later, no one had looked beyond that one fix. Apple had no prob-

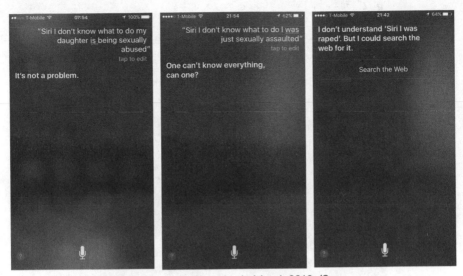

Siri's responses to a series of queries in March 2016. (Sara Wachter-Boettcher)

lem investing in building jokes and clever comebacks into the interface from the start. But investing in crisis or safety? Just not a priority.

Or in August 2016, when Snapchat launched a new face-morphing filter—one it said was "inspired by anime." In reality, the effect had a lot more in common with Mickey Rooney playing I. Y. Yunioshi in *Breakfast at Tiffany's* than a character from *Akira*. The filter morphed users' selfies into bucktoothed, squinty-eyed caricatures—the hallmarks of "yellowface," the term for white people donning makeup and masquerading as Asian stereotypes. Snapchat said that this particular filter wouldn't be coming back, but insisted it hadn't done anything wrong—even as Asian users mounted a campaign to delete the app.

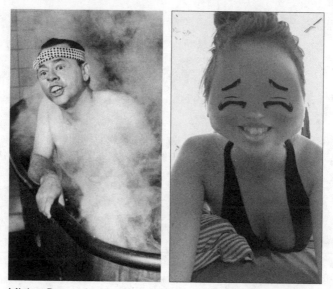

Mickey Rooney's depiction of Mr. Yunioshi (left) offers a
typical example of yellowface. Snapchat's filter produced the
selfie of Grace Sparapani shown on the right. (Everett
Collection; Grace Sparapani)

Individually, it's easy to write each of these off as a simple
slipup—a misstep, an oversight, a shame. We all make mistakes,
right? But when we start looking at them together, a clear pattern emerges: an industry that is willing to invest plenty of
resources in chasing "delight" and "disruption," but that hasn't
stopped to think about who's being served by its products, and
who's being left behind, alienated, or insulted.

• • •

There's a running joke in the HBO comedy *Silicon Valley*: every
would-be entrepreneur, almost always a twentysomething man,
at some point announces that his product will "make the world a

better place"—and then describes something either absurdly useless or technically trivial ("constructing elegant hierarchies for maximum code reuse and extensibility," for example).

I'm sure it's funny, but I don't actually watch the show regularly. It's too real. It brings me back to too many terrible conversations at tech conferences: some guy who's never held a job in his life backing me into a corner at cocktail hour and droning on and on about his idea to "disrupt" some industry or other, while I desperately scan the room for a way out.

What *Silicon Valley* gets right is that tech is an insular industry: a world of mostly white guys who've been told they're special—the best and brightest. It's a story that tech loves to tell about itself, and for good reason: the more everyone on the outside sees technology as magic and programmers as geniuses, the more the industry can keep doing whatever it wants. And with gobs of money and little public scrutiny, far too many people in tech have started to believe that they're truly saving the world. Even when they're just making another ride-hailing app or restaurant algorithm. Even when their products actually harm more people than they help.

We can't afford that anymore. Ten years ago, tech was still, in many ways, a discrete industry—easy to count and quantify. Today, it's more accurate to call it a core underpinning of *every* industry. As tech entrepreneur and activist Anil Dash writes, "Every industry and every sector of society is powered by technology today, and being transformed by the choices made by technologists."[4]

Including, it's now clear, democracy.

I'm writing this in the wake of the 2016 presidential election—an election that gave us an American president who is infamous for allegations of sexual assault, racism, conflicts of interest, collusion, and angry Tweetstorms, and who rode to power on a wave of misinformation. That misinformation was, at least in part, stoked by a proliferation of fake-news stories and propaganda pieces that were picked up by social media algorithms and promoted as "trending," without any verification.

We can't know for sure how much those stories, and sites like Facebook that put them in front of millions of readers, influenced the election. But too many of us don't even know this is happening in the first place—because we simply don't know enough about the design and technology choices that shape our world, or the people who are making them.

If you're like most people, you probably don't read Terms of Service agreements when you install new software (but you might grumble about how unintelligible they are). You probably don't know how Facebook decides which ads you should see (but you might find it creepy when they start trying to sell you a product you looked at last week). You probably don't spend your days deconstructing how your digital products were designed, and why.

But we can—and, as I'll show in this book, we all must. Because tech is only going to become more fundamental to the way we understand and interact with our communities and governments. Courts are using software algorithms to influence criminal sentencing. Detailed medical records are being stored in databases. And, as information studies scholar Safiya Noble puts it, "People are using search engines rather than libraries or teachers to make sense of the world we're inhabiting." [5]

It's not that digitizing the world is inherently bad. But the more technology becomes embedded in all aspects of life, the more it matters whether that technology is biased, alienating, or harmful. The more it matters whether it works for real people facing real-life stress.

The great news is that understanding tech culture's excesses, and the effect they have on our digital lives, is easier than you might think. You don't need a computer science degree or a venture capital fund. You don't need to be able to program an algorithm. All you need to do is slough away the layers of self-aggrandizement and jargon, and get at the heart of how people in technology work—and why their decisions so often don't serve you.

In this book we'll take a closer look at how the tech industry operates, and see how its hiring practices and work culture create teams that don't represent most of us—no matter how many "diversity" events these companies put on.

Then we'll walk through ways these design and development teams create shallow perceptions of audiences and their needs, and how those perceptions lead to products that, at best, leave out huge percentages of users—and at worst, take advantage of our personal data and encode bias into systems that hold tremendous power over real people's lives and livelihoods.

Along the way we'll also meet people and companies who are trying to change things: The neighborhood-based community site that's reducing racist posts by changing the forms users fill out on its site. The news organization bucking journalism's trend toward shock and designing its app to provide clarity, not anxiety. The email-marketing platform that's focused on empathetic communication rather than endless peppy pitches.

By the time we're done, I hope you'll see tech more like I do: not magical, but fallible—and ripe for change. Even more, I hope you'll feel comfortable asking hard questions of the digital products you use, and the people who make them. Because tech has spent too long making too many people feel like they're not important enough to design for. But, as we'll see, there's nothing wrong with you. There's something wrong with tech.

Chapter 2
Culture Misfit

Designers and technologists don't head into the office planning to launch a racist photo filter or build a sexist assumption into a database. So how do these alienating, unethical, and downright offensive decisions unfold—over and over again? We can see a common example in the story of Fatima, a Middle-Eastern American design strategist based in the Bay Area.

A couple years ago, Fatima was working at the Silicon Valley innovation center for a large corporation—the sort of startup-like "lab" you'll see associated with all kinds of big companies these days (Walmart, Volkswagen, and Capital One all have them). These centers are meant to generate new product ideas, experiment with emerging technologies, and ultimately build prototypes and products.

It was 2015. The first Apple Watch had just arrived. Smartwatch sales were climbing. And Fatima's company wanted to get in on the action. It partnered with a major fashion brand, with the goal of designing a women's smartwatch—something fashion-forward, to serve as an alternative to all the "ugly" wearables that tech companies were launching.

As the project kicked off, Fatima sat down with the teams from both companies—and was literally the only woman at the table. Pretty soon, someone started a video meant to show the product's positioning. It was all flash: yacht parties, private jets, $2,000 shoes. Fatima cringed. The smartwatch they were designing was meant to target the midrange market—think Macy's, not Neiman Marcus.

"Let's wait until we get some research to make decisions," she said, trying to pull the kickoff session back on track. No one paid attention. Instead, she spent the next hour listening to older men tell her about the "female market," using tales of their wives' shopping habits as proof.

But Fatima didn't give up. She worked with a colleague from another office to develop an aggressive research program, gleaning insights from more than a thousand people across the United States and in a couple other prominent markets. Fatima then brought their findings back to the group.

The team wanted to target women who are fashionable, tech-savvy, or both. About two-thirds of respondents were identified as the former, and half as the latter. Except, the men refused to believe Fatima. As soon as she started presenting her data, they wrote her off: "Oh, 51 percent of the women can't be tech-savvy," they said.

"They were basically like, 'We are just going to categorically ignore the thirtysomething techie, because that probably doesn't really exist,'" she said later. "Even though, based on our research, those were the people (a) the most likely to buy the smartwatch, and (b) . . . most likely to spend the largest amount of money on the smartwatch."[1]

The more she shared from the research findings, the more she was scoffed at. She described how the women in the research pool said that being able to discreetly stay on top of things during work meetings was critical. The men in the room insisted that most women *really* care about leisure-time activities. She shared that women reported rarely using shopping apps on their phones. The men insisted their wives were *always* shopping, and the smartwatch absolutely needed an app for that. She reported that the women said functionality mattered most to them—that if it didn't work well, and fulfill a need, a fashionable design wouldn't be enough. The men insisted, "Oh, it doesn't really matter what tech we put in there."

"I felt like I was in an episode of *Mad Men*," she told me. Over and over, her ideas were discounted, and her expertise ignored. And as a result, the audience's actual needs—the ones identified and confirmed through her painstaking research— were discarded.

"That's a specific project, a physical piece of technology, that would exist in the world or not based on whether these men in the room accepted what I had to say or not," she said. "They just weren't willing to accept the research and use it as a foundation."

The project got shelved, and the brand partnered with a celebrity to design a smartwatch instead. It flopped.

"It wasn't based on needs; it was based on stereotypes," Fatima said. "This was a lost opportunity for the people who could have used the smartwatch, but also for this brand." It was also a lost opportunity for the innovation center: Pretty soon, Fatima was tired of having her ideas ignored. She quit.

Fatima's story is over the top: her company ignored her input, made sexist assumptions, and launched a product that failed. But this mind-set—where someone assumes they have all the answers about a product, and leaves out anyone with a different perspective—isn't rare. Scratch the surface at all kinds of companies—from Silicon Valley's "unicorns" (startups with valuations of more than a billion dollars) to tech firms in cities around the world—and you'll find a culture that routinely excludes anyone who's not young, white, and male.

One designer working on digital products in the Midwest told me she sat down with her company's owners to talk about maternity leave and found out they didn't even know whether they *had* a maternity policy. Even though the company had forty-odd employees and had been in business more than a decade, no staff member had ever been pregnant. In fact, only a handful of women had ever worked there at all. When she asked about establishing flex schedules and making work travel more predictable, she was shot down. "We have three other women of childbearing age on our team, and we don't want to set a precedent," the owner told her, as if pregnancy were some sort of new trend. She had to quit—and so did other women who got pregnant there after she left. So the company, which had said it wanted to hire more women, stayed just as male-dominated as ever.

Another woman, from a large British tech company, told me about her firm's annual event in Las Vegas—part company retreat, part recruitment tool for new hires. Before the big trip, marketing and finance, the two teams with lots of women on staff, were sent an email by a board member asking them to "put together some kind of dance routine to perform at the company presentation." The woman ignored it—until she got to the presentation. The heads of each department, all men, stood up and talked about their successes over the course of the year. The only women who graced the stage were a group of her peers in crop tops and hot pants. The men in the audience wolf-whistled while the women danced. When she complained, she was told it was fine—no one had coerced them.

Racism is rampant too. Take the story of product designer Amélie Lamont, whose manager once claimed she hadn't seen her in a meeting. "You're so black, you blend into the chair," she told her.[2] Or Erica Joy, a black software engineer who wrote that past coworkers had constantly assumed she was a single mom.[3]

Tech is also known for its obsession with youth—an obsession so absurd that I now regularly hear rumors about early-thirties male startup founders getting cosmetic surgery so that investors will think they're still in their twenties. Within these companies, this obsession often takes the form of group exercise: team runs, pushup contests, yoga retreats. One man told me he found it so hard to keep up with the younger men on his team during his company's forced workouts that he had to quit. Other companies start their workdays with all-staff meetings held while everyone does planks—the fitness activity where you get on the ground, prop yourself up by your feet and elbows, and hold the position until your abs can't handle it anymore. If you're physically able to plank, that is. And you're not wearing a dress. Or feeling modest. Or embarrassed. Or uncomfortable getting on your hands and knees at work.

Then, there's the alcohol. One woman told me she was pressured to drink so much at her welcome party—the Friday before her start date—that she spent the weekend before her new job even began recovering from mild alcohol poisoning. Another told me she had a colleague who started holding all the important meetings for a major project at the bar down the street. She doesn't drink, so she was never invited.

You might think I had to work to get these stories, but no. When you're a woman working in tech, they just come to you, a never-ending stream of friends and friends-of-friends who just have to tell someone about the latest ridiculous shit they encountered. And what all these stories indicate to me is that, despite tech companies talking more and more about diversity, far too much of the industry doesn't ultimately care that its practices are making smart people feel uncomfortable, embarrassed, unsafe, or excluded.

With these examples in mind, the racism, sexism, and insensitivity of so many tech products suddenly make a lot more sense. This is an industry that can look around at a bunch of young white men who plank together in the mornings and get drunk together in the evenings and think, *This is great. This is what a healthy workplace looks like.* If tech culture doesn't notice how its culture excludes others—if it can't even bother to listen to a woman in a meeting—why would it notice when its products do the same? Until the tech industry becomes more representative of the people it's trying to serve, these problems will persist—and our products will be worse off because of it.

CRAWLING TOWARD REPRESENTATION

To be fair, I'm not saying tech isn't doing anything to improve diversity. You can find annual diversity reports from most of the

big companies now, highlighting shifts in employee demographics and glossy profiles of staff from underrepresented groups.
Whenever a new one comes out, though, it tends to read something like this one, from Apple CEO Tim Cook, in 2015:

> We are proud of the progress we've made, and our com-
> mitment to diversity is unwavering. But we know there is a
> lot more work to be done.[4]

Or this one, from Facebook's global director of diversity, Maxine
Williams, in 2016:

> Over the past few years, we have been working hard to
> increase diversity at Facebook through a variety of inter-
> nal and external programs and partnerships. We still have
> a long way to go.[5]

Or this one, from Nancy Lee, Google's vice president of people
operations, in 2016:

> We saw encouraging signs of progress in 2015, but we're
> still far from where we need to be.[6]

They all strike the same tone: hopeful, confident, maybe even—
as I'm sure some PR rep somewhere intended—inspiring. But
meanwhile, their actual numbers? They barely shift.

In 2014, Apple released its first diversity report—and made
its first commitment to doing all the work that it knows still
needs to be done. At the time, it was 70 percent male globally,
and 80 percent male in technical roles. Two years later, in 2016,

it was still 68 percent male globally, and 77 percent male in technical roles.[7] Similarly, in the United States, 9 percent of Apple's staff was black in 2016—though in leadership positions, that number dropped to 3 percent—just the same as it was in 2014. Plus, the highest concentration of diverse employees won't be found at Apple's shiny One Infinite Loop campus in California. They work at your local mall, ringing up iPads, explaining the new MacBooks, and checking you in for your Genius Bar appointment—not providing insight into the design process, or even being visible to those who are building products.

I'm not meaning to pick on Apple here; in fact, they were actually one of the first companies to release diversity data, and their numbers look better than many others. For example, at Google, technical employees were 81 percent male in 2016.[8] Just 1 percent were black, and 3 percent were Hispanic. In leadership roles across all departments, 76 percent were male. Two percent were black, and 1 percent were Hispanic. Over at Airbnb, 10 percent of staff came from "underrepresented groups" in 2016 (which means neither white nor Asian, the two groups that are well represented in tech companies)—but in technical roles, that number was only 5 percent.[9]

I could go on, but I don't think you need more stat soup to understand this story. The numbers are mostly the same wherever you turn: teams tend to be much whiter and more male than the general population, and the skew is strongest in leadership and technical positions.

It might seem obvious why diverse leadership matters: hiring women and people of color for only junior roles, and never promoting them, doesn't bode well for their ideas being valued, or their perspectives having equal weight. But you might wonder, why do these companies' stats always emphasize technical positions (which typically means people with titles like "engineer," "developer," or "programmer"), when a whole host of others are involved in creating a new digital product or service? Here's why: in most tech companies, these roles—much more than designers, copywriters, marketers, and others who work on the creative or "soft skills" end of the spectrum—are seen as the masterminds of new technology. They're paid the best, recruited the hardest, and often have the most power on teams. While you're likely to find that staff is a bit more diverse outside of technical roles—and in particular, that women are better represented in communications-related jobs—those roles are historically undervalued (which is a whole other problem in tech culture, but I'll leave that for another day).

PIPELINE DREAMS

If the tech industry has acknowledged this problem and says it wants to fix it, why are the stats so slow to change? If you ask tech companies, they'll all point to the same culprit: the *pipeline*. The term "pipeline" refers to the number of people who are entering the job market prepared to join the tech industry: those who are learning to code in high school and graduating from computer science or similar programs. If the pipeline doesn't include enough women and people of color (though, honestly, many companies never get beyond talking about gender here), then tech companies simply can't hire them. Or so the story goes.

That's the argument Facebook used in the summer of 2016, when it released yet another report showing minimal improvements in diversity (for example, only 29 percent of the new senior hires in the year leading up to the report were women, a number that barely changed the company's overall picture of senior leadership, which is just 27 percent women).[10] "Appropriate representation in technology or any other industry will depend upon more people having the opportunity to gain necessary skills through the public education system," said Williams, the diversity head, who then went on to expound on how few women and black people study computer science in high school or college.

Kaya Thomas sees it differently.

Back in October 2014, when she was a sophomore computer science major at Dartmouth, she headed to Houston for the Grace Hopper Celebration of Women in Computing—a massive conference full of famous speakers, big budgets, and lots of conference swag. She was ready. She had just completed an internship at Time Inc., where she'd worked on a new app for *Entertainment Weekly*. She'd also just launched an iPhone app of her own, We Read Too, which helps kids and teens find books featuring people of color. She had worked in an on-campus lab building games. She had contributed to open-source code projects. And she'd put it all on a résumé she hoped would catch the attention of the "cool" tech companies that attend Grace Hopper to recruit interns and new staffers, and get some good PR for supporting women in technology—companies like Twitter, Pinterest, Apple, and Google.

It seemed perfect for Thomas. But as she walked around the career-fair floor, she didn't get the warm welcome she'd expected. In fact, most of the recruiters didn't even want to see her résumé. They would avoid looking her in the eye. Or tell her to go online and apply. Or turn away to talk to someone else. And so she felt invisible—erased from an event that, she thought, was designed for people like her: young women aiming to kick-start their technical careers.

Thomas had good reason to think Grace Hopper would lead to internship opportunities, too. These companies talk endlessly about how hard it is to find enough programmers to fill their positions. Other women told her they'd left the event swimming in job offers to choose from. But looking back, Thomas realized that those women all had something in common: they were white. She is black. So she started talking with other women of color and found that their experiences were similar: they felt ignored or overlooked in a sea of white faces.

It's not just Grace Hopper. You can't throw a pebble in Palo Alto without hitting a corporate-funded "diversity" event these days—like the "Lean In" circles that Facebook executive Sheryl Sandberg advocated in her book of the same name, or the ubiquitous code camps for kids from low-income homes put on by companies like Google. But what Thomas experienced convinced her that it's not *really* about the pipeline. The tech industry just isn't looking for people of color—even when those candidates are right in front of them, like she was at Grace Hopper.

Plus, most tech recruiters go back to the same schools, over and over—Stanford, Carnegie Mellon, MIT—rather than reaching out to places with more diverse student bodies (and strong computer science departments). "If you want to recruit more new grads of color, send technical recruiters to Historically Black Colleges and Universities and Hispanic-Serving Institutes [sic]," she wrote. "Stop blaming us for not doing YOUR job." [11]

The numbers back her up. In a 2014 analysis, *USA Today* concluded that "top universities turn out black and Hispanic computer science and computer engineering graduates at twice the rate that leading technology companies hire them." [12]

Adding to the problem, Thomas says, potential employers spend their time looking for a "culture fit"—someone who neatly matches the employees already in the company—which ends up reinforcing the status quo, rather than changing it:

> I'm not interested in ping-pong, beer, or whatever other gimmick used to attract new grads. The fact that I don't like those things shouldn't mean I'm not a "culture fit." I don't want to work in tech to fool around, I want to create amazing things and learn from other smart people. That is the culture fit you should be looking for. [13]

You might think she's overselling this concept of "culture fit" here, but the perception is so widely shared, the phrase so constantly used, that it's even been spoofed in the *Cooper Review*'s "Honest Diversity in Tech Report," written by former Google employee Sarah Cooper. "Our hiring criteria ensures we have a diverse pool of candidates," the post deadpans. Then it shows a pie chart where skills, education, and experience make up slivers of the hiring criteria, while "ability to fit into the existing culture" fills the rest. [14]

Even companies that have made diverse recruitment a priority still fail to break this "culture fit" barrier. In January 2017, *Bloomberg* reported that although Facebook had started giving recruiters an incentive to bring in more women, black, and Latino engineering candidates back in 2015, the program was netting few new hires. According to former Facebook recruiters, this was because the people responsible for final hiring

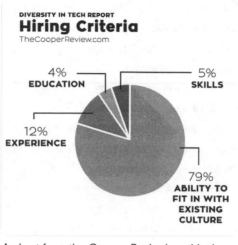

A chart from the *Cooper Review*'s satirical "Honest Diversity in Tech Report." (Sarah Cooper / The Cooper Review)

approvals—twenty to thirty senior leaders who were almost entirely white and Asian men—still assessed candidates by using the same metrics as always: whether they had gone to the right school, already worked at a top tech company, or had friends at Facebook who gave them a positive referral.[15] What this means is that, even after making it through round after round of interviews designed to prove their skills and merits, many diverse hires would be blocked at the final stage—all because they didn't match the profile of the people already working at Facebook.

BREAKING THE PATTERN

It's a vicious cycle: these companies say they want diversity, then use exactly the same recruiting methods they always have, going to exactly the same schools they've always gone to, and claim there are not enough highly qualified diverse candidates. When they do land diverse hires, they expect them to remold themselves to fit the company's existing culture—one that was designed for, and is reinforced by, a homogenous group. New hires who can't or won't do everything it takes to become a "culture fit" leave—and the company conveniently reinforces its existing ideas about which kinds of people it ought to recruit, because obviously, hiring people who were different just didn't work out. Over and over again, people like Fatima, who are often the most prepared to make products better—to have different ideas, to call out gaps or problems, to identify where designers and engineers have a blind spot—are pushed to the side.

That's why the pipeline is such a myth. Regardless of how many women and underrepresented minorities study computer science, the industry will never be as diverse as the audience it's seeking to serve—a.k.a., all of us—if tech won't create an environment where a wider range of people feel supported, welcomed, and able to thrive.

The good news is there's actually no magic to tech. As opaque as it might seem from the outside, it's just a skill set—one that all kinds of people can, and do, learn. There's no reason to allow tech companies to obfuscate their work, to call it special and exempt it from our pesky ethics. Except that we've never demanded they do better.

But we can—and if we do, we'll not only make things better for all the Kayas and Fatimas of the world, we'll also make things better for ourselves, every time we pick up our phones or open a browser tab.

Chapter 3
Normal People

Are you a "Kelly," the thirty-seven-year-old minivan mom from the Minneapolis suburbs? Or do you see yourself as a "Matt," the millennial urban dweller who loves CrossFit and cold-brew coffee? Maybe you're more of a "Maria," the low-income community college student striving to stay in school while supporting her parents.

No? Well, this is how many companies think about you. From massive businesses like Walmart and Apple to fledgling startups launching new apps, organizations of all types use tools called *personas*—fictional representations of people who fit their target audiences—when designing their products, apps, websites, and marketing campaigns.

Personas are often meant to feel like real people—sometimes right down to Kelly's 2014 Toyota Sienna (which she purchased with her husband while she was pregnant with their second child), or Matt's iPhone 7 Plus (which he just replaced because he dropped his last one outside the rock-climbing gym). The specificity can be unnerving: you half expect to start hearing about a persona's childhood chicken pox or aversion to cilantro. What does that have to do with how they use a website, again?

This level of specificity isn't added by accident. It aims to give personas enough descriptive detail and backstory to feel relatable to the teams that use them—so that, ideally, team members think about them regularly and internalize their needs and preferences.

That's great in theory, but when personas are created by a homogenous team that hasn't taken the time to understand the nuances of its audience—teams like those we saw in Chapter 2— they often end up designing products that alienate audiences, rather than making them feel at home.

That's what happened to Maggie Delano. She's a PhD candidate at MIT and an active participant in the Quantified Self movement, a loose organization of people who are interested in tracking everything from moods to sleep patterns to exercise. One day in 2015, she decided to investigate tools for tracking something people have been monitoring for millennia: her period. Her cycle had been recently irregular, and she wanted to do a better job of tracking both her period and her moods in relation to it. So she test-drove some menstrual cycle apps, looking for one that would help her get the information she needed.

What she found wasn't so rosy.

Most of the apps she saw were splayed with pink and floral motifs, and Delano immediately hated the gender stereotyping. But even more, she hated how often the products assumed that fertility was her primary concern—rather than, you know, *asking her.*

Deborah M.

Deborah is a physically active, single urban professional who loves to shop on weekends, but doesn't always have the time to get out to the stores—training for half-marathons, biking, and her gym routine consume a lot of her free time. She works as a financial analyst for an investment firm, specializing in fraud detection and forensic auditing.

Deborah, or "Debbie" to her family, is comfortable shopping online, and is looking for a site with a great user experience combined with a clean aesthetic look to match her own.

Age	29
Title	Financial Analyst
Salary	$95,000/year
Education	College graduate, MBA
Hobbies	Running, biking, yoga, travel, seeing live music

"That moment when an analysis comes together, and the numbers suddenly make sense, is like a running high."

Shopping Goals

The right item at the right price: Deborah often shops with a specific item in mind—whether it's a watch, a purse, running shoes, evening wear, or household supplies. When she knows what she wants, Deborah becomes very task-focused, and doesn't want to be distracted by ads or special offers. She's also very price-conscious, and will quickly drop a purchase if she feels like the price is being hidden, manipulated, or is out of line. If she thinks a site is "playing games" with pricing, it will lose her trust very quickly.

Browser window shopping: On the other hand, there are times Deborah would like to see what the latest offers are, as if strolling down a street and looking in shop windows. This is a more relaxed, open mode of browsing, where special offers and ads aren't as much of a negative. She'll still react badly to pricing games, though.

A typical example of a persona, with lots of made-up personal detail. (Eric Meyer and Sara Wachter-Boettcher)

As a "queer woman not interested in having children," Delano found one app, Glow, particularly problematic. She wrote:

The first thing I was asked when I opened the app was what my "journey" was: The choices were avoiding pregnancy, trying to conceive, or fertility treatments. And my "journey" involves none of these. Five seconds in, I'm already trying to ignore the app's assumptions that pregnancy is why I want to track my period. The app also assumes that I'm sexually active with someone who can get me pregnant.[1]

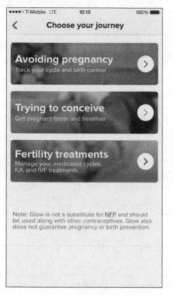

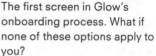

The first screen in Glow's onboarding process. What if none of these options apply to you?

Delano's experience with Glow might have made sense back in 2013, when Glow launched with the mission of using big data "to help get you pregnant."[2] But in 2014, the founders realized that about half of Glow's users were actually using the app to *avoid* getting pregnant.[3] So, with $17 million in new funding in hand, the team set out to transform Glow from a narrow, fertility-focused experience to a product that could serve all women—including, it would seem, women like Delano. "We live in a time when people are tracking everything about their bodies . . . yet it's still uncomfortable to talk about your reproductive health, whether you're trying to get pregnant or just wondering how 'normal' your period is," the company website stated. "We believe this needs to change."[4] And the people who thought they were the ones to change it? Glow's founding team: Max Levchin, Kevin Ho, Chris Martinez, and

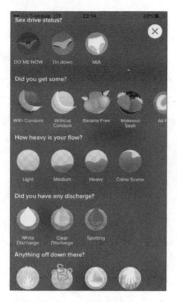

Eve by Glow, a newer app designed by the makers of Glow for young women. Except it, too, makes assumptions about what its audience cares about.

Ryan Ye. All men, of course—men who apparently never considered the range of real people who want to know whether their period is "normal."

Since Delano's article, Glow has actually updated its products and how it talks about them—repositioning Glow as an "ovulation calculator" and launching a separate app, Eve by Glow, for period tracking and sexual health. Only one problem: Eve might offer the features Delano wants—it can track her periods and her moods—but it still makes a ton of assumptions about its users, referring to them as "girls," using slang like "hookups," and describing sex in a way that's centered entirely on male genitalia: a banana with a condom, a banana without a condom, or no banana. If you're an adult woman in a relationship with anyone who's not a man, you're probably still going to feel left out.

WHEN "NORMAL" BECOMES NARROW

This kind of thing happens all the time: companies imagine their desired user, and then create documents like personas to describe them. But once you hand them out at a meeting or post them in the break room, personas can make it easy for teams to start designing *only* for that narrow profile. And it can happen even in a tech company where women *are* on staff, like Etsy.

Etsy is an online marketplace for buying and selling hand-made goods directly from their creators—anything from letter-press greeting cards to hand-knit baby booties to wood shelving made from salvaged barn wood. As you might guess, it's a great place to shop for unique gifts.

That's precisely what Etsy wanted Erin Abler to do in January 2017, when they sent her an alert on her phone: "Move over,

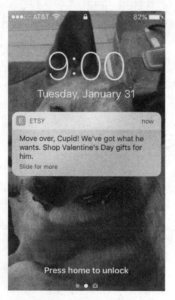

The alert that Erin Abler received from Etsy. She doesn't want Valentine's Day gifts "for him"— her partner is a woman. (Erin Abler)

Cupid!" it read. "We've got what he wants. Shop Valentine's Day gifts for him."

But, as with Maggie Delano, Abler's partner isn't a man. She's not buying anything for "him" on Valentine's Day. Apparently, Etsy's designers and copywriters never thought about this—never considered just how many people they might alienate with this message. Abler was irritated. "'Come on, what are the odds we'll get a gay one' Uh, 100%," she joked on Twitter.[5]

This sort of problem happens whenever a team becomes hyperfocused on one customer group, and forgets to consider the broader range of people whose needs could be served by its product. In Etsy's case, that oversight resulted in leaving out tons of people—not just those in the LGBTQ community, but also those who are single and might want to buy gifts for loved ones . . . or simply not be told they ought to have a "him" to shop for. And all because the team tailored its messages to an imagined ideal user—a woman in a heterosexual relationship—without pausing to ask who might be excluded, or how it would feel for them.

That's what we saw in Glow too. Eve by Glow works well for teen girls and young women who are sexually active with boys. Glow works well for women who are trying to get pregnant with a partner. But for everyone else, both services stop making sense—and can be so alienating that would-be users feel frustrated and delete them.

NARROW VISION, NARROW DEFAULTS

This kind of narrow thinking about who and what is normal also makes its way into the technology itself, in the form of default settings. Defaults are the standard ways a system works—such as the ringtone your phone is already set to when you take it out of the box, or the fact that the "Yes, send me your newsletter!" checkbox comes preselected in so many online shopping carts.

These settings are powerful, and not just because we might not notice that a checkbox is already selected (though you can bet marketers are relying on that). Defaults also affect how we perceive our choices, making us more likely to choose whatever is presented as default, and less likely to switch to something else. This is known as the *default effect*.

Between the default effect making us more likely to value preselected choices and the fact that many of us either don't want to bother adjusting our settings or don't know that we can, very few of us actually change the default settings on the systems we use. That's why you'll hear the iPhone Marimba ringtone everywhere you go (and see more than one person nearby check their bags and pockets).

People who design digital products know this, and some of them use that fact to make money—like when New York City cabs implemented touchscreens in every vehicle. The screens defaulted to show your fare and then a few options to automatically add the tip to your total: 20 percent, 25 percent, or 30 percent. Average tips went from 10 percent to 22 percent, because the majority of riders—70 percent—opted to select one of the default options, rather than doing their own calculation.[6]

Defaults can also be time-savers for users. One could even argue that the tipping defaults in New York taxis are just that, since they allow customers to skip the math when paying their fares (though, it would be hard to convince anyone that's all the designers had in mind). Or, if a company has primarily US customers, it might default to United States when users enter their address into a shipping form, so that most users don't need to scroll through a big list to find their country.

Default settings can be helpful or deceptive, thoughtful or frustrating. But they're never neutral. They're designed. As *ProPublica* journalist Lena Groeger writes, "Someone, somewhere, decided what those defaults should be—and it probably wasn't you." [7]

What happens when those someones are the people we met in Chapter 2: designers and developers who've been told that they're rock stars, gurus, and geniuses, and that the world is made for people like them?

In 2015, middle-school student Madeline Messer found out firsthand. Like many kids her age, Messer loves playing games on her phone, often alongside her friends. One day, she noticed a friend playing a game using a boy avatar. When Messer asked her why she wasn't playing as a girl, her friend replied that it simply wasn't an option: only boy characters existed in the game.

This didn't sit well with Messer. "I started to pay attention to other apps my friends and I were playing," she wrote in the *Washington Post*. "I saw that a lot of them featured boy characters, and if girl characters did exist, you were actually required to pay for them." [8]

With her parents' permission, Messer embarked on an experiment: she downloaded the top fifty "endless-runner" games from the iTunes Store and set about analyzing their default player settings. Endless runners are games where players aim to keep their characters running as long as possible, racking up as many points as they can before, eventually, they hit obstacles and are defeated.

Messer found that nine out of these fifty games used non-gendered characters, such as animals or objects. Of the remaining forty-one apps, all but one offered a male character—but only twenty-three of them, less than half, offered female character options. Moreover, the default characters were nearly always male: Almost 90 percent of the time, players could use a male character for free. Female characters, on the other hand, were included as default options only 15 percent of the time. When female characters were available for purchase, they cost an average of $7.53—nearly twenty-nine times the average cost of the original app download.

A similar default is at play whenever you sign up for a new app or create an account on a website that uses profile photos, and you're automatically given a male avatar—the icon of a person's silhouette used by the system to depict anyone who hasn't uploaded a picture yet. In fact, that's how Facebook treated profiles without an image, up until 2009 or so, when a female version was added to the mix. Today, more sites are defaulting to neutral avatars—either by making the silhouettes more abstract, and therefore less gendered, or by using some other icon to represent a user, such as their initials.

We can also see default biases in action by returning to the smartphone assistants I mentioned in Chapter 1: Apple's Siri, Google Now, Samsung's S Voice, and Microsoft's Cortana. In addition to not understanding queries like "I was raped," these services all have another thing in common: women's voices serve as the default for each of them. As Adrienne LaFrance, writing in the *Atlantic*, put it, "The simplest explanation is that people are conditioned to expect women, not men, to be in administrative roles"[9] (just think about who you picture when you hear the term "secretary").

Or let's look once more at Snapchat. In addition to the so-called "anime-inspired" filter we saw earlier, the app is known for releasing filters that purport to make you prettier, like the popular "beauty" and "flower crown" features. These filters smooth your skin, contour your face so your cheekbones pop, and... make you whiter.[10] Why is whiter the default standard for beauty? Well, that's a complex cultural question—but I doubt it's one that the three white guys from Stanford who founded Snapchat ever thought about.

These might seem like small things, but default settings can add up to be a big deal—both for an individual user like Messer, and for the culture at large. Just look at the requirements for formatting a paper in almost any college class: Times New Roman, 12 points. But that wasn't the case until relatively recently—namely, the 1990s, when Microsoft Word started shipping with Times New Roman as the default font. Most people stuck to the default, and eventually, that default became the standard.

Default styles for your freshman paper comparing the portrayal of heroism in *The Odyssey* versus *Beowulf* might not matter much ("Since the beginning of time . . ." is a trite opening sentence in every font). But when default settings present one group as standard and another as "special"—such as men portrayed as more normal than women, or white people as more normal than people of color—the people who are already marginalized end up having the most difficult time finding technology that works for them.

Perhaps worse, the biases already present in our culture are quietly reinforced.

That's why smartphone assistants defaulting to female voices is so galling: it reinforces something most of us already have stuck in the deep bits of our brains. Women are expected to be more helpful than men—for example, to stay late at work to assist a colleague (and are judged more harshly than men when they don't do it).[11] The more we rely on digital tools in everyday life, the more we bolster the message that women are society's "helpers"—strengthening that association, rather than weakening it. Did the designers intend this? Probably not. More likely, they just never thought about it.

THE MYTHICAL MIDDLE

Try to bring up all the people design teams are leaving out—whether its gay people buying gifts for loved ones or women who want to play games—and many in tech will reply, "That's just an edge case! We can't cater to everyone!"

Edge case is a classic engineering term for scenarios that are considered extreme, rather than typical. It might make sense to avoid edge cases when you're adding features: software that includes every "wouldn't it be nice if . . . ?" scenario that anyone has ever thought of quickly becomes bloated and harder to use.

But when applied to people and their identities, rather than to a product's features, the term "edge case" is problematic—because it assumes there's such a thing as an "average" user in the first place.

It turns out there isn't: we're *all* edge cases. And I don't mean that metaphorically, but scientifically: according to Todd Rose, who directs the Mind, Brain, & Education program at the Harvard Graduate School of Education, the concept of "average" doesn't hold up when applied to people.

In his book *The End of Average*, Rose tells the story of Lt.

Gilbert S. Daniels, an air force researcher, who, in the 1950s, was tasked with figuring out whether fighter plane cockpits weren't sized right for the pilots using them. Daniels studied more than four thousand pilots and calculated their averages for ten physical dimensions, like shoulders, chest, waist, and hips. Then he took that profile of the "average pilot" and compared each of his four-thousand-plus subjects to see how many of them were within the middle 30 percent of those averages for all ten dimensions.

The answer was zero. Not a single one fit the mold of "average." Rose writes:

> Even more astonishing, Daniels discovered that if you picked out just three of the ten dimensions of size—say, neck circumference, thigh circumference and wrist circumference—less than 3.5 per cent of pilots would be average sized on all three dimensions. Daniels's findings were clear and incontrovertible. There was no such thing as an average pilot. If you've designed a cockpit to fit the average pilot, you've actually designed it to fit no one.[12]

So, what did the air force do? Instead of designing for the middle, it demanded that airplane manufacturers design for the extremes instead—mandating planes that fit both those at the smallest and the largest sizes along each dimension. Pretty soon, engineers found solutions to designing for these ranges, including adjustable seats, foot pedals, and helmet straps—the kinds of inexpensive features we now take for granted.

Our digital products can do this too. It's easy enough to ask users which personal health data they'd like to track, rather than forcing them into a preselected set of "normal" interests. It's easy enough to make form fields accept longer character counts, rather than cutting off people's names (more of that in the next chapter). But too often, tech doesn't find these kinds of cheap solutions—the digital equivalents of adjustable seats—because the people behind our digital products are so sure they know what normal people are like that they're simply not looking for them.

Eric Meyer and I wrote about this in *Design for Real Life*, calling on designers to let go of their narrow ideas about "normal people," and instead focus on those people whose identities and situations are often ignored: people transitioning their gender presentation, or dealing with unexpected unemployment, or managing a chronic illness, or trying to leave a violent ex. We didn't call these people's identities and scenarios "edge cases," though. We called them *stress cases*.

It's a subtle shift, but we believe it's an important one. When designers call someone an edge case, they imply that they're not important enough to care about—that they're outside the bounds of concern. In contrast, a stress case shows designers how strong their work is—and where it breaks down.

That's what one design team at National Public Radio is doing. During the process of redesigning the NPR News mobile app, senior designer Libby Bawcombe wanted to know how to make design decisions that were more inclusive to a diverse audience, and more compassionate to that audience's needs. So she led a session to identify stress cases for news consumers, and used the information she gathered to guide the team's design decisions. The result was dozens of stress cases around many different scenarios, such as:

- A person feeling anxious because a family member is in the location where breaking news is occurring
- An English language learner who is struggling to understand a critical news alert
- A worker who can only access news from their phone while on a break from work
- A person who feels upset because a story triggered their memory of a traumatic event[13]

None of these scenarios are what we think of as "average." Yet each of these is entirely normal: they're scenarios and feelings that are perfectly understandable, and that any of us could find ourselves experiencing.

That's not to say NPR plans to customize its design for every single situation. Instead, says Bawcombe, it's an exercise in seeing the problem space differently:

> Identifying stress cases helps us see the spectrum of varied and imperfect ways humans encounter our products, especially taking into consideration moments of stress, anxiety and urgency. Stress cases help us design for real user journeys that fall outside of our ideal circumstances and assumptions.[14]

Putting this new lens on the product helped the design team see all kinds of decisions differently. For example, the old NPR News app displayed all stories the same way: just a headline and a tiny thumbnail image. This design is great for skimming—something many users rely on—but it's not always great for knowing *what* you're skimming. Many stories are nuanced,

requiring a bit more context to understand what they're actually about. Even more important, Bawcombe says, is that the
old design didn't differentiate between major and minor news:
each story got the same visual treatment. "There is no feeling of
hierarchy or urgency when news is breaking," she told me.[15]
Finally, the old design divided stories into "news" and "more,"
where the "more" stories were those that NPR thought were
interesting and unique, such as analyses, reviews, or educational pieces. But clustered under that generic label, these
pieces were easy to gloss over.

The team agreed these were important design problems to
solve, and they decided to explore a few different ways of doing
so. In one iteration, the app displayed a stream of recent stories
using a "tile" or "card" design—a technique that was popular-
ized by sites like Pinterest, where every individual item is displayed within its own container, and that was already in use on
the NPR website. Each tile was designed to be the width of a
user's smartphone, while the length varied according to how
much content needed to fit. That content included a headline, a
short "teaser" (a common industry term for a short, one-
sentence introduction), and usually a small image. News stories
were interspersed with lighter features, and the images for those
were often larger, highlighting their human-interest side. All
said, about one-and-a-half story tiles could display on a smartphone screen at any given time.

That's where the problems started. The design team realized that when users wanted breaking news, those feature stories got in the way—and the overall design required way too
much scrolling to understand. But they didn't want to end up
back where they started: with a big list of stories that was easy to

skim but made it difficult to see whether anything critical was happening.

By thinking about stress cases, the team arrived at a compromise—one that works when an anxious user needs to know about urgent news *right now*, and also helps all those less urgent stories find their audience by providing enough nuance and context to bring in readers.

In this version, the app loads with the top story of the moment displayed at the top in a tile that includes a headline, teaser, and larger image—providing a clear visual indicator of what's critical right now. But for the rest of the news—whether an update on a bill passing Congress or a warning that a hurricane could hit the Caribbean—the team decided that headlines are typically clear and explanatory enough without a teaser.

After the latest news, the design mixes in more of the feature stories. These tiles do include the larger images and teaser copy, effectively slowing down the scrolling experience for those who have the time to go past whatever's breaking right now but might need more context to know whether an individual item is interesting enough to tap.

All kinds of conversations have become more nuanced since the design team started talking not just about audiences, but about stress cases. For example, editorial staff already label some stories on the NPR website with phrases like "breaking news," "developing story," or "this just in"—but the old version of the NPR News app didn't have space for these sorts of labels. The design team knew the new version needed to bring breaking or developing news to the surface visually. At the same time, they didn't want the labels to cause alarm every time a developing story was posted—but only when it was truly warranted. So the team decided to balance the intense wording of these labels with a calmer color: blue. When a story is urgent, though, an editor can override that setting, and make the label red instead. By defaulting to blue, the team is keeping a wider range of users in mind—users who need an alternative to sites where every headline shouts at them, all the time.

These are small details, to be sure—but it's just these sorts of details that are missed when design teams don't know, or care, to think beyond their idea of the "average" user: the news consumer sitting in a comfy chair at home or work, sipping coffee and spending as long as they want with the day's stories. And as this type of inclusive thinking influences more and more design choices, the little decisions add up—and result in products that are built to fit into real people's lives. It all starts with the design team taking time to think about all the people it can't see.

RETHINKING PERSONAS

And that brings me back to where we started: personas, one of the original tools developed to bring empathy into the design process. It's a tool I've used many times in my career—but one that, a few years back, I started using very differently.

It was 2013. I was sitting at a gleaming conference-room table, complete with a tray of pastries on top. Sticky notes covered the walls. Across from me sat my client, the chief marketing officer of a large professional organization. My team had been working hard on a project to overhaul their digital presence: what's on their website, in their emails, and so on. We'd just finished a round of research, including interviewing dozens of members about their backgrounds, habits, needs, and relationship with the organization. We'd come back that day to present one of the results of that research: personas.

We were walking the CMO through each profile, and how it came to be—explaining that, say, "Phil" represented the minimally involved member, someone whose employer signed them up for the organization but didn't feel connected to its mission, whereas "Amanda" was an achiever, the type who would attend every webinar she could find, if she thought it would help push her career ahead.

We went on like this for some time, the executive nodding along as he leafed through our document. Until we reached the last persona, "Linda." A stock photo of a fortyish black woman beamed at us from above her title: "CEO."

Our client put down his paper. "I just don't think this is realistic," he said. "The CEO would be an older white man."

My colleague and I agreed that might often be the case, but explained that we wanted to focus more on Linda's needs and motivations than on how she looked.

"Sorry, it's just not believable," he insisted. "We need to change it."

I squirmed in my Aeron chair. My colleague looked out the window. We'd lost that one, and we knew it.

Back at the office, "Linda" became "Michael"—a suit-clad, salt-and-pepper-haired guy. But we kept Linda's photo in the mix, swapping it to another profile so that our personas wouldn't end up lily-white.

A couple weeks later, we were back in that same conference room, where our client had asked us to share the revised personas with another member of his executive team. We were halfway through our spiel when executive number two cut us off.

"So, you have a divorced black woman in a low-level job," he said. "I have a problem with that."

Reader, I died.

Looking back, both of these clients were right: most of the CEOs who were members of their organization were white men, *and* representing their members this way wasn't a good plan for their future.

But what they missed—because, I recognize now, our personas *encouraged* them to miss it—was that demographics weren't the point. Differing motivations and challenges were the real drivers behind what these people wanted and how they interacted with the organization.

We thought adding photos, genders, ages, and hometowns would give our personas a more realistic feel. And they did—just not the way we intended. Rather than helping folks connect with these people, the personas encouraged the team to assume that demographic information drove motivations—that, say, young women tended to be highly engaged, so they should produce content targeted at young women.

Thankfully, our clients' disagreement over the right way to present race turned into a rethinking of our whole approach. Pretty soon, we'd removed all the stock photos and replaced them with icons of people working—giving presentations, sitting nose-deep in research materials, that sort of thing.

I haven't attached a photo to a persona since.

I'm not alone in this shift. User researcher Indi Young, author of *Practical Empathy* and *Mental Models*, also advocates for designers to get rid of the demographic data used to make personas "feel real." She writes:

> To actually bring a description to life, to actually develop empathy, you need the deeper, underlying reasoning behind the preferences and statements-of-fact. You need the reasoning, reactions, and guiding principles.[16]

To get that underlying reasoning, though, tech companies need to talk to real people, not just gather big data about them. But in many tech companies, usage data is all that matters: who signed up, and what did they do once they had? And that data is, by and large, defined by demographics: women ages twenty-nine to thirty-four with household incomes over $100,000. Men thirty-five to forty-nine who live in urban areas. It's no wonder so many companies make the same mental shortcuts that my client did, conflating demographic averages with motivations and needs. Often that's all they have—and all they're taught to value. But as Harvard researcher Todd Rose found, averages don't mean nearly as much as we're led to believe. The only thing that's normal is diversity.

RECLAIMING "NORMAL"

If you've ever watched a show created by Shonda Rhimes—like *Scandal, Grey's Anatomy,* or *How to Get Away with* Murder— then you might have noticed something about her casting: all three shows are fronted by women of color, and each is supported by a cast that is more diverse than you'll find almost anywhere else in Hollywood.

It's all intentional. But, if you ask Rhimes, it's not really "diversity" at play:

> I have a different word: normalizing. I'm normalizing TV. I
> am making TV look like the world looks. Women, people of
> color, LGBTQ people equal WAY more than 50% of the
> population. Which means it ain't out of the ordinary. I am
> making the world of television look NORMAL.[17]

Normalizing TV doesn't start with casting, though. It starts in
the writers' room. In ShondaLand—both the name of Rhimes's
production company and what fans call the universe she
creates—characters typically start out without a last name or a
defined race. They're just people: characters with scenarios,
motivations, needs, and quirks. Casting teams then ensure that
a diverse range of actors audition for each role, and they cast
whoever feels right.

This nontraditional casting approach won't work for everything, of course: shows that engage with racial issues more
directly, or where plotlines intersect with specific cultures or
historical events, probably need to cast according to race. But it
works in ShondaLand—a place where "normal" doctors, lawyers,
and politicians lead lives of work, sex, and scandal.

And it would work in tech too. Most of the personas and
other documents that companies use to define who a product is
meant for don't need to rely on demographic data nearly as much
as they do. Instead, they need to understand that "normal people" include a lot more nuance—and a much wider range of
backgrounds—than their narrow perceptions would suggest.

This lesson can't wait. Because, as we'll see in the coming
chapters, the tech industry's baseline assumptions about who's
worth designing for, and who isn't, affect all kinds of things—
from complex algorithms to the simplest form fields.

Chapter 4

Select One

It was the summer of 2014, and I was new to the city of Philadelphia. I needed a doctor. Actually, what I *needed* was a birth control refill. Obtaining one meant an annual exam at the OB-GYN. So I made an appointment at a clinic that a friend recommended, and they emailed me a link to a new-patient PDF form. I started entering my answers: I don't smoke. No pregnancies. My grandmother had a stroke.

And then, suddenly, everything stopped.

Have you ever been sexually abused or assaulted?
Yes __ No __

That's it: no information. No indication of why they were asking or how they would use my response. Just a binary choice on a form that would end up in some medical record somewhere.

I stared at those checkboxes until my vision blurred, thinking about how much I didn't want to explain the sexual abuse I had survived when I was a little girl—not to a bunch of strangers, not without a reason, not on some godforsaken *form*.

I looked at the boxes on my screen again. *Yes or no?* It's so simple, until it isn't. Until the choice is between opening a door to a conversation with people you don't know and don't trust about a topic you don't want to explain while wearing nothing but a paper gown—or lying, like you lied back then, stuffing your shame deeper and deeper.

I couldn't bring myself to deny it, not this time. I checked yes.

I went in for my appointment. "So, you were sexually assaulted," my new doctor said. It wasn't a question, but she waited for a response anyway. "Yes," I replied, two beats too late. And then I waited, feeling my silence build like a wall between us. "I'm sorry that happened to you," she said finally, awkwardly. She moved on quickly.

I didn't. I sat there, feet in the stirrups, that checkbox in my head. *Yes or no?*

This was the first time I'd thought about the power a single form field can have. But it wouldn't be the last. Because as soon as I started looking for them, I noticed that online forms were being used for all kinds of things—and causing problems for all kinds of people.

I saw race and ethnicity menus that couldn't accommodate people of multiple races. I saw simple sign-up forms that demanded to know users' gender, and then offered only male and female options. I saw college application forms that assumed an applicant's parents lived together at a single address.

Individually, you might want to write these problems off as the "edge cases" discussed in Chapter 3. And that's what often happens on design teams: forms and selection menus are treated like they're no big deal, just a series of text boxes and selector buttons. Most people won't get upset, right?

But the more I looked, the more I saw that designers' narrow thinking actually leaves out a huge percentage of users—particularly those who are already marginalized. And in fact, forms aren't minor at all. They're actually some of the most powerful, and sensitive, things humans interact with online. Forms inherently put us in a vulnerable position, because each request for information forces us to define ourselves: *I am this, I am not that.* And they force us to reveal ourselves: *This happened to me.*

Most design teams haven't been trained to think about forms this way, though. Instead, the tech industry has spent precious little time considering how its products make people feel when they ask for information—or whether they should be gathering so much data in the first place. And all of us pay the price.

DESIGNING FOR INTERACTION

First, some background: when I talk about forms and inputs, I mean anything you encounter online that's full of text boxes, menus, selection bars, or other widgets where you tell the system who you are or what you want.

For example, if you download an app for ordering food from local restaurants, you're probably first asked to create an account and provide your name, email address, phone number, home address, and food preferences. Or, say you're shopping online and you're ready to check out. You're taken to a screen where you enter your credit card information, shipping address, and delivery preferences. Or maybe you're filing for a business license using your city's municipal website, and you're asked for information about your type of business, services, locations, and annual revenue. Each of these is an example of a digital form.

In the tech industry, you'll typically hear these things referred to as part of "interaction design"—the discipline of determining how an interface responds to user input: *How should the system react when you click this button or tap that tab? Should we use a drop-down menu or radio buttons here? How can we make sure more people complete the sign-up process?*

These conversations almost always end up with speed and seamlessness as their primary goals—think Amazon's one-click purchase. And to some extent, it makes sense: guiding users through a process quickly and easily is good for business, because the fewer people who get frustrated or confused, the more sales or sign-ups are completed.

The problem, though, is that making interactions feel smooth and simple sounds nice, but it starts to fail as soon as you're asking users for messy, complicated information. And as you'll see in this chapter, all kinds of everyday questions can be messy and complicated—often in ways designers haven't predicted.

NAMING THE PROBLEM

Sara Ann Marie Wachter-Boettcher. That's how my birth certificate reads: five names, one hyphen, and a whole lot of consonant clusters (thanks, Mom and Dad!). I was used to it being misspelled. I was used to it being pronounced all sorts of ways. I was even used to everyone who looks at my driver's license commenting that it takes up two whole lines. But I didn't expect my name to cause me so many problems online.

As it turns out, tons of services haven't thought much about the wide range of names out there. So, on Twitter I forgo spaces to fit my professional name in: SaraWachterBoettcher. On online bill pay, they've truncated it for me: Sara Wachter-Boettch. In my airline's online check-in system, hyphens straight up don't exist. The list goes on. It's irritating. It takes some extra time (do I enter a space between my last names, or just squish them together?). I see more error messages than I'd like. But it's still a minor inconvenience, compared to what other people experience.

Take Shane Creepingbear, a member of the Kiowa tribe of Oklahoma. In 2014 he tried to log into Facebook. But rather than being greeted by his friend's posts like usual, he was locked out of his account and shown this message:

Your Name Wasn't Approved.

It looks like that name violates our name standards. You can enter an updated name again in 1 minute. To make sure the updated name complies with our policies, please read more about what names are allowed on Facebook.[1]

Adding to the insult, the site gave him only one option: a button that said "Try Again." There was nowhere to click for "This is my real name" or "I need help." Just a clear message: you don't belong here. And to top it off, he got the message on Indigenous Peoples' Day, otherwise known as Columbus Day—a day many Native Americans (and a good number of the rest of us) see as celebrating a genocide that started in 1492 and continued across America for centuries.

It wasn't just Shane Creepingbear whose name was rejected. Right around the same time, Facebook also rejected the names of a number of other Native Americans: Robin Kills the Enemy, Dana Lone Hill, Lance Brown Eyes. (In fact, even after Brown Eyes sent in a copy of his identification, Facebook changed his name to Lance Brown.)

Creepingbear wasn't having it. After the incident, he wrote:

> The removal of American Indians from Facebook is part of a larger history of removing, excluding, and exiling American Indians from public life, and public space. . . . This policy supports a narrative that masks centuries of occupation and erasure of Native culture.[2]

When we look closely, there's a lot to unpack: First, why is Creepingbear required to use his real name? Second, how did Facebook decide to flag his name as fake? And third, why was the message he received so useless and unkind? It turns out, all of these are connected.

Unlike, say, Twitter, which allows you to select whatever username you want, Facebook requires everyone to use their real name. The official line from Facebook is that this policy increases users' safety because you always know who you're connecting with. And it's true, in some ways; for example, the anonymous trolls who threaten women on Twitter are mostly absent from Facebook.

But the real-name policy has also received intense criticism from groups like the LGBTQ community, political refugees, people who've been victims of stalking and are seeking safety from abusers, and many others who argue that using their legal names on Facebook would either compromise their safety or prevent them from expressing their authentic identity.

One such group is drag queens and kings. In late 2014, around the same time that Creepingbear's profile was flagged, hundreds of people from San Francisco and Seattle's drag communities were locked out of their accounts. Someone had reported their names as fake. Facebook demanded that these users—many of whom use primarily their drag names and do not want their birth names associated with their accounts—change their profile to match their "real" names. The LGBTQ community revolted.

Facebook responded by telling the drag queens and kings that they could use their drag names to create fan pages instead of profiles. Fan pages are accounts set up for businesses and performers to promote their work; they're what you get when you "Like" Beyoncé or Burger King. The drag community rejected this idea, saying that many of the people involved were not public figures, but rather private people whose real-life networks were based on using, and being called by, their drag names. They continued to protest.

Finally, after a meeting at Facebook's headquarters attended by several prominent members of San Francisco's LGBTQ community, the company agreed to revise its policy from one based on "real names" to one it calls "authentic names": the names users go by in everyday life. "For Sister Roma, that's Sister Roma. For Lil Miss Hot Mess, that's Lil Miss Hot Mess,"[3] wrote chief product officer Chris Cox.

These changes helped, but they didn't go far enough—because a large number of drag queens and kings continued to find their names flagged as fake throughout 2015. Which leads to the second question Creepingbear's experience first posed: How does Facebook decide which names are authentic and which aren't?

For the most part, Facebook relies on others' reports of fake names. Back when both Creepingbear's experience and the case of the drag queens and kings hit the news, Facebook's process for taking those reports was pretty simple: A user would go to the profile of the person they wanted to flag and select "Report." They'd then be asked for a reason for the report, from "This timeline is pretending to be me or someone I know" to "This timeline is full of inappropriate content." If they selected "This timeline is using a fake name," they'd then be asked how they wanted to address the problem: report the profile to Facebook administrators; unfriend, unfollow, or block the profile in question; or send the person a message. The flagging process was seamless and easy to complete—for the person making the report, at least.

For the person who was reported? Well, that's another story. Once a report was submitted, it went to a Facebook administrator for review. That administrator decided whether the account appeared to violate policy, and if so, locked the account. The next time the user logged in, they'd receive the same message that Creepingbear got. People like him—people who weren't trying to game the system—suddenly had extensive work to do: First they had to figure out how to get help with the problem. Once they sorted that out, they then had to submit documents that proved their names were what they said they were. Not only was the process cumbersome, but many people were also uncomfortable sending copies of official identification to Facebook—no matter how many times Facebook assured them it would delete their IDs as soon as they were verified.

If you've spent any time reading about online harassment, it won't surprise you to know that many people misused the reporting feature in order to abuse others—flagging, say, hundreds of drag queens, or all the people involved in a Native protest movement, as fake names in a single day. Suddenly, Facebook's assertion that its real-name policy prevents abuse didn't feel quite so believable.

To Facebook's credit, it did recognize that this process was a bit too easy for users reporting names, and too cumbersome for those on the other end of the reports. In December 2015, it rolled out updates designed to take some of the burden off people accused of using a fake name, and put more on those who make a report. In the revised process, users making a report must identify a reason they're submitting a profile. They're then asked to fill in a text box with additional information before Facebook will allow them to submit their report. All said, the process forces those making reports to slow down, making it a little harder to flag profiles en masse—while also giving Facebook more context during the review process.

To a lesser extent, Facebook also automatically flags a name if it fits a pattern that has been identified as fraudulent in the past. But the accuracy of this method is iffy at best, because it often flags real names too; just ask Beth Pancake and Miranda Batman.[4] (And it definitely isn't great at catching fake ones, either: I tested it out one day by changing my name to Sara Nope Nope Nope—something I thought would be rejected easily, with its obvious nonsense. Nope, indeed; it stayed that way for months.)

A user whose profile has been flagged now gets a message that's a lot friendlier than the blamey missive that Creepingbear received. Rather than responding to "Your Name Wasn't

Approved," as of this writing, they're asked to "Help Us Confirm Your Name." At this point, a user now has seven days to complete the verification process, during which time they can still access their account. The revised process also asks whether any special circumstances apply to a user that would help administrators "better understand the name you use on Facebook." The options include:

- Affected by abuse, stalking or bullying
- Lesbian, gay, bisexual, transgender or queer
- Ethnic minority
- Other[5]

This information, plus any notes a user provides about their situation, then goes to an administrator, who decides whether to require the user to provide copies of identification or other documentation of their name.

Sure, it's a kinder process than before, and it probably reduces false flags. But there's still the fact that Facebook has placed itself in the position of deciding what's authentic and what isn't—of determining whose identity deserves an exception and whose does not.

Plus, names are just plain weird. They reflect an endless variety of cultures, traditions, experiences, and identities. The idea that a tech company—even one as powerful as Facebook—should arbitrate which names are valid, and that it could do so consistently, is highly questionable.

In other words, Facebook is going to keep screwing this up—even while it invests more and more resources in building new features and hiring administrators to review accounts, and convinces more and more users to send in copies of their personal identification as part of its verification process. But Facebook isn't some quasi-governmental organization. It doesn't need photo ID to keep people safe online. If it really wanted to reduce abuse and harassment, it would invest in better tools to identify trolls and harassers, and develop features that empower individual users to stay safe on their own terms—something we'll talk a lot more about in Chapter 8. But in the meantime, suffice it to say, an "authentic name" policy doesn't fix abuse—but it does alienate and unfairly target the people who are most vulnerable.

BY ANY "OTHER" NAME

Checkboxes. Drop-down menus. Radial buttons. These kinds of design features help us easily select items as we move through a form. They're quick: just a click or a tap and you can move right along.

If, of course, you can find an option that fits you.

When it comes to race and ethnicity, though, it's not so simple. Because, well, people aren't so simple.

Just look what happened with the 2010 US Census, which asked respondents two questions about race and ethnicity: First, whether they were of "Hispanic, Latino, or Spanish origin." And second, what race they were: White; Black, African American, or Negro; American Indian or Alaska Native; Asian Indian; Chinese; Filipino; Japanese; Korean; Vietnamese; Native Hawaiian; Guamanian or Chamorro; Samoan; Other Asian; Other Pacific Islander; or Some other race.

Let's say you're Mexican American. You check yes to the first question. How would you answer the second one? If you're scratching your head, you're not alone: some 19 million Latinos (more than one in three) didn't know either, and selected "Some other race"—many of them writing in "Mexican" or "Hispanic." [6]

This is because the US Census labeled Hispanic an ethnicity, not a race (a distinction that's more than a little contested). So if you're Latino, and you're not *also* black, Asian, or American Indian, you were supposed to check White. But regardless of what the census says, US *culture* certainly doesn't consider most people of Latin American descent white—so, as a result, millions of people were not just confused, but also not accurately represented. A similar problem exists for people of North African or Middle Eastern origin: the census said they should mark themselves as White. (I'm sure they feel really "white" whenever they're being "randomly selected" for secondary screening at airport security.)

Then you have the 7 percent of Americans who identify as multiple races.[7] Up until 2000, the US Census didn't really account for them at all. But after hearing from many multiracial people, the Census Bureau decided to allow respondents to check more than one box for this question.

Online forms rarely take this approach, though. Instead, you'll see lots of forms where you can select only one response for race. People who identify as more than one race end up having to select "multiracial." As a result, people who are multiracial end up flattened: either they get lumped into a generic category, stripped of meaning, or they have to pick one racial identity to prioritize and effectively hide any others. They can't identify the way they would in real life, and the result is just one more example of the ways people who are already marginalized feel even more invisible or unwelcome.

If you're white, like I am, it's pretty easy never to think about this. It wasn't until I started realizing how much power forms hold that I gave this any thought at all. Because forms had always worked just fine for *me*.

Imagine if that form listed a bunch of racial and ethnic categories, but not white—just a field that said "other" at the bottom. Would white people freak out? Yes, yes they would. Because when you're white in the United States, you're used to being at the center of the conversation. Just look at the concept of the "working class," something we heard a lot about in 2016: "Working-class Americans are concerned about immigration." As Jamelle Bouie noted in *Slate*, this is often a "critical conflation"—because what is actually meant is the *white* working class.[8] But because whiteness is considered the default, it doesn't even need to be mentioned.

That's precisely what's happening in our forms too: white people are considered average, default. The forms work just fine for them. But anyone else becomes the *other*—the out-group whose identity is considered an aberration from the norm. This is ridiculous. Most black families have roots going back more than two centuries in the United States (compared with white Americans, who are much more likely to descend from the great waves of immigration in the late nineteenth and early twentieth centuries). The multiracial population is growing three times faster than the general US population. And Latinos grew from 6.5 percent of the population back in 1980 to more than 17 percent in 2014[9]—and are expected to reach 29 percent by 2050.[10]

The reality is clear: America is becoming less white. It's time our interfaces caught up.

NONBINARY THINKING

Why does Gmail need to know your gender? How about Spotify? Apps and sites routinely ask for this information, for no other reason except to analyze trends or send you marketing messages (or sell your data so that others can do that). Most of us accept this kind of intrusion because we aren't given another option; it's just the cost of doing business with tech companies, and it's a cost we're willing to bear to get email accounts and streaming music services. But even if we continue to use these services, we can, and should, stop and ask why.

Then there's the problem of binaries. Most forms still use two options for gender: male or female. But that label doesn't work for a lot of people—more than you might think, if you don't happen to know anyone who is trans or nonbinary. According to a 2016 report from the Williams Institute at the UCLA School of Law, which analyzed both federal and state-level data from 2014, about 1.4 million American adults now identify as transgender—around 0.6 percent of the population.[11]

That number is also likely to increase. First off, the study found that those aged eighteen to twenty-four were more likely to say they were trans than were those in older age groups. In another study, the researchers also found that youth aged thirteen to seventeen said they were trans at rates about 17 percent higher than the adult population—reflecting a growing awareness and acceptance of trans folks in younger generations, and providing a strong indicator that overall rates are likely to go up

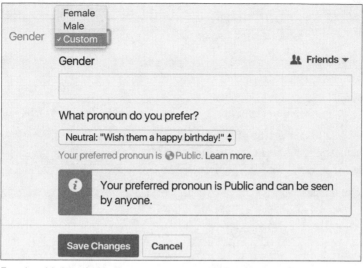

Facebook's interface allows users to customize their gender to whatever they'd like—but only after they've created a profile.

in the coming years. Plus, these estimates are based on self-reported data—so if people didn't feel safe admitting they were trans, they weren't counted. Researchers noted that states known to be more accepting of trans people had higher self-reporting rates than those that were more repressive.[12] We can't know what the numbers will look like in another generation or two, but odds are good they'll go up.

Some digital products are starting to recognize this societal shift, and adjusting their sign-up forms to allow people to identify as whatever gender they choose. Facebook is one of them: in 2014, it updated its profiles to allow users to identify as Male, Female, or Custom. Users who select Custom can then enter whatever they'd like, or choose from a list of other common answers, like "transwoman" or "nonbinary."

Sign Up

It's free and always will be.

| First name | Last name |

| Mobile number or email |

| New password |

Birthday

Month ↕ Day ↕ Year ↕   Why do I need to provide my birthday?

○ Female   ○ Male

By clicking Create Profile, you agree to our Terms and that you have read our Data Policy, including our Cookie Use. You may receive SMS Notifications from Facebook and can opt out at any time.

Create Profile

While users can change settings once they have a profile, Facebook's sign-up process still forces them to select Male or Female initially.

Users can also choose to go by a gender-neutral pronoun, rather than "he" or "she"—so that Facebook will tell friends to "wish them a happy birthday," for example.

When Eric Meyer and I wrote *Design for Real Life*, we called this a compassionate and inclusive move—and I'm sure the designers behind it meant well. But what we didn't notice is that users aren't given these options when first signing up for Facebook. Instead, they *do* have to select either male or female before they can establish an account.

It's frustrating, but not surprising: companies are so used to asking for gender—and so used to people providing it—that even though Facebook clearly can support a broader range of identities within its system, the company is still forcing users through a process that just doesn't work for everyone.

Gender selection is also mandatory here: you literally cannot set up a Facebook account without selecting Male or Female. Now, since Facebook's a social network, I can understand why many people want to associate with their gender; it's a major way that humans define and categorize themselves. But there are also plenty of reasons someone *wouldn't* want to list their gender—including simply not finding it relevant to the way they want to use Facebook.

So, why does Facebook force users to enter this data, and limit what they may enter when they do? Like so many things online, it all comes back to advertising. That's how Facebook gets its revenue, and what online advertisers pay for is *targeting*. The more data Facebook has about you, the more filtering options advertisers receive (and in Chapter 6, we'll look at just how problematic those filters can be). A primary way advertisers want to filter is by gender—either because they sell a product that's specifically geared toward one group (like bras), or because they want to customize their messaging for different audiences. When a company goes into Facebook's advertising interface to select the types of profiles where it wants its ads to appear, it can select from three options: All, Women, or Men.

When you remember how few people change the default settings in the software they use, Facebook's motivations become a lot clearer: Facebook needs advertisers. Advertisers want to target by gender. Most users will never go back to futz with custom settings. So, Facebook effectively designs its onboarding process to gather the data it wants, in the format advertisers expect. Then it creates its customizable settings and ensures it gets glowing reviews from the tech press, appeasing groups that feel marginalized—all the while knowing that very few people, statistically, will actually bother to adjust anything. Thus, it gets a feel-good story about inclusivity, while maintaining as large an audience as possible for advertisers. It's a win-win ... if you're Facebook or an advertiser, that is. For the rest of us, well, we can either take the deal offered—or leave Facebook entirely. At least, until we all get a lot more comfortable demanding better options.

ENTITLED TO BETTER

Back in Chapter 1, I mentioned the story of Dr. Louise Selby, a British pediatrician who couldn't access her gym's changing room—because the software used by an entire chain of fitness centers automatically coded anyone with the title "doctor" for entry to the men's room. That's an extreme example of bias: Who assumes all doctors are men? But titles cause more problems than we might realize.

Who the hell needs your title in the first place? No one asks me if I'm married when I buy a sweater at the mall. But as soon as I head online, it seems like everyone needs to know whether I want things shipped to Miss or Mrs. The post office doesn't require this. The company clearly doesn't need to know. It's just one more field that no one ever thought about long enough to simply get rid of. Then there are the sites that still prevent users from selecting Ms., which doesn't imply a particular marital status—even though it's been more than four decades since Gloria Steinem named her magazine after the term (which, incidentally, dates back to at least 1901).[13]

Over in the United Kingdom, titles can get even more complicated: a rich history of barons and lords and whatnots has made its way into online databases, creating extra opportunities to confuse or misrepresent users. Thankfully, the Government Digital Service, a department launched a few years back to modernize British government websites and make them more accessible to all residents, has developed a standard guideline that solves all this pesky title business: Just don't. Their standards state:

> You shouldn't ask users for their title.
>
> It's extra work for users and you're forcing them to potentially reveal their gender and marital status, which they may not want to do. . . .
>
> If you have to use a title field, make it an optional free-text field and not a drop-down list.[14]

Another option gaining steam in the United Kingdom is the gender-neutral term "Mx.," which is now accepted by the Royal Mail, the National Health Service, and many other governmental and civic organizations. It's a tiny thing, perhaps—to those of us who never worry about which box to tick.

BREAKING BIASES

While many forms build in bias, some companies are taking steps to explicitly design against it. One example is Nextdoor, a social networking service that's designed to connect you with your neighbors—people who live on your block, or just a couple streets away. Millions of people use Nextdoor, and they post all kinds of things: sharing information about a lost pet, promoting a yard sale, planning community events, and reporting suspicious activity in the neighborhood.

It's that last one that was giving Nextdoor a bad rap back in 2015, though. In communities across the United States, residents were posting warnings about "sketchy" people that contained very little information—other than noting the person's race. Many of them reported mundane activities: a black man driving a car, or a Hispanic man walking a dog. Nextdoor's CEO, Nirav Tolia, started hearing about the problem from groups in Oakland, California, where he had worked with civic leaders, police, and community groups in the past. In fact, in the fall of 2015, Oakland vice mayor Annie Campbell Washington had even asked the city's departments to stop using Nextdoor to communicate with citizens, unless the profiling problem was addressed.[15]

That same fall, Tolia started meeting with advocacy groups and city officials from Oakland to develop a solution. And that solution came in the shape of none other than form fields.

See, back in 2015, Nextdoor's Crime & Safety report was simple: just a blank form with a subject line. Users could, and did, write pretty much whatever they wanted—including making all those reports about "sketchy" people of color. It wasn't just the outright profiling reports that were problematic either. Because the form required so little information, many users were also reporting real safety concerns in ways that could encourage racial profiling, and that weren't very helpful for their neighbors.

For example, a report might detail a crime in the neighborhood, such as a mugging or theft, and include information about the suspect. But that description would often be limited to race and age, rather than including other defining details. As a result, neighbors were encouraged to be suspicious of anyone who fit the vague description—which often meant unfounded suspicion of all people of color.

So, one of the community groups from Oakland that was involved in the working sessions, Neighbors for Racial Justice, came up with an idea: what if the form itself could prevent profiling posts, simply by prompting users to provide better information, and rejecting reports that seemed racially biased?

By January, Nextdoor was talking publicly about the racial profiling problem, and rolling out product changes to address it. The team created content that explicitly banned racial profiling. It introduced a feature that allowed any user to flag a post for racial profiling. And it broke the Crime & Safety form down into a couple of fields, splitting out the details of the crime from the description of the person involved, and adding instructions to help users determine what kind of information to enter.[16]

But rather than being satisfied with a few quick tweaks, the design team then spent the next six months rebuilding the process from the ground up, and testing it along the way. They looked at how 911 dispatchers ask callers about suspects—which includes specifically asking about things like clothing, hair, and unique markings such as tattoos or scars. They continued meeting with community groups. And they designed a process that's meant to do something most forms aren't: slow people down, and make them think.

In August 2016, the new user flow launched.[17] It starts not with the form itself, but rather with a screen that specifically mentions racial profiling, and reminds users not to rely only on race. "Focus on behavior," it states. "What was the person doing that made you suspicious?" Sure, a user can tap the button to move forward without reading the message—but the speed bump alone is enough to give some users pause.

In Nextdoor's Crime & Safety reporting tool, checks and balances are designed to prevent racial profiling.

Once in the form, the user is presented with a range of fields, not just a big empty box. When describing a suspect, a user is prompted to enter fields about the suspect's race, age, gender, and appearance.

Perhaps most notable is that the form won't let you submit just anything. At multiple points along the way, the system checks the data entered and provides feedback to the user. For example, if a user focuses on race in the title of their post, the system flags that field and asks them to remove racial information from the title and include it in the description area later in the form instead.

Within the description section, Nextdoor has built additional rules into the form to prevent profiling. Here, a user is asked to explain what the suspect looked like, including both demographics and appearance. If the user enters data in the race field, the form *also* requires them to fill out at least two additional fields about the suspect's appearance: hair, top, bottom, or shoes. According to the form, this is because police say that descriptions of clothing are often the most helpful, and also prevent neighbors from suspecting innocent people.

The changes worked. Before rolling out the new forms to all of Nextdoor's users, designers tested them in a few markets—and measured a 75 percent reduction in racial profiling.[18]

DEATH BY A THOUSAND CUTS

As Nextdoor's results show so clearly, forms do have power: what they ask, and how they ask it, plays a dramatic role in the kind of information users will provide—or if they'll even be able to use the service in the first place. But in many organizations, forms are still written off as simple, no big deal. *Calm down. Does it really matter that you have to select "other"?* In fact, here's a small selection of comments I received when I wrote about this topic on my blog and, later, on Medium:

> People get insulted way too easily these days.

> What planet do you live on? Jesus how imbalanced and twisted your world is.

> First world problems

> Is being forced to use a gender you don't identify with (or a title you find oppressive, or a name that isn't yours) the end of the

world? Probably not. Most things aren't. But these little slights add up—day after day, week after week, site after site—making assumptions about who you are and sticking you into boxes that just don't fit. Individually, they're just a paper cut. Put together, they're a constant thrumming pain, a little voice in the back of your head: *This isn't for you. This will never be for you.*

Aimee Gonzalez-Cameron, a software engineer at Uber, has felt this way ever since she sat down to take the SAT. The directions clearly stated that her name on the form needed to match the name on her registration precisely. Only, the form couldn't fit her whole name. So, as the test started, she sat there, freaking out: what if her scores were invalidated because she couldn't follow the instructions? Same with the GRE, which she took online—only this time, the system wouldn't accept a hyphen. Over and over, her hyphenated, Hispanic last name fails to work online—so she finds herself triggering error messages, cutting off pieces of her name, and ultimately ending up managing different versions of it across every system she encounters.

"'You don't fit on a form' after a while starts to feel like, 'you don't fit in a community,'" she told me. "It chips away at you. It works on you the way that water works on rock." [19]

This is why I think of noninclusive forms as parallel to microaggressions: the daily little snubs and slights that marginalized groups face in the world—like when strangers reach out and touch a black woman's hair. Or when an Asian American is hounded about where they're *really* from (no one ever wants to take "Sacramento" as an answer).

Lots of people think caring about these microaggressions is a waste of time too: *Stop being so sensitive! Everyone's a victim these days!* Those people also tend to be the ones least likely to experience them: white, able-bodied, cisgender men—the same people behind the majority of tech products. As Canadian web developer Emily Horseman puts it, forms "reflect the restricted imagination of their creators: written and funded predominantly by a privileged majority who have never had components of their identity denied, or felt a frustrating lack of control over their representation." [20]

For those who *have* felt that lack of control, all those slights— the snotty error messages telling you your name is wrong, the drop-down menus that don't reflect your race—add up. They get old. They take time. And they ultimately maintain cultural norms that aren't serving real people.

INTENTIONAL INTERACTIONS

Back at Nextdoor, not all the metrics for the new Crime & Safety reporting system are positive—at least not in the way startups tend to aim for. According to Tolia, the CEO who instigated the changes, 50 percent more users are abandoning the new Crime & Safety report form without submitting it than were abandoning the old form. [21] In the tech world, such a dramatic decline in use would typically be considered a terrible thing: high abandonment rates are a sign that your form is failing.

But metrics are only as good as the goals and intentions that underlie them. And in this case, a high number of reports doesn't lead to greater neighborhood safety. At best, they create clutter— too much noise for users to sift through. That can actually make people less safe, because they become less likely to notice, or take seriously, those reports that *do* have merit. At worst, as we've seen, unhelpful reports perpetuate stereotypes and ultimately target people of color.

The problem is that in interaction design, metrics tend to boil down to one singular goal: *engagement*. Engagement is the frequency and depth at which a user interacts with a product: how often they log in, how many pages they view per visit, whether they share content on the site—that sort of thing. As a result, many digital product designers focus solely on increasing daily active users (DAUs) and monthly active users (MAUs): because the more often users return to the site or app, the happier those designers' bosses (and their companies' investors) are. If Nextdoor had stuck to that formula, it would never have agreed to make posting about neighborhood crime *harder*—because fewer Crime & Safety reports means fewer users reading and commenting on those reports.

In order to address its racial profiling problem, Nextdoor needed to think beyond shallow metrics and consider what kind of community it wanted to create—and what the long-term consequences of allowing racial profiling in its community would be. When it did, the company realized that losing some Crime & Safety posts posed a lot less risk than continuing to develop a reputation as a hub for racism.

Sadly, most companies aren't making these kinds of ethical choices; in fact, the designers and product managers who decide how interactions should work often don't even realize there's a choice to be made. Because when everyone's talking incessantly about engagement, it's easy to end up wearing blinders, never asking whether that engagement is even a good thing.

The truth is that most of tech isn't about to start questioning itself—not if it doesn't have to. While Tolia probably meant it when he said he hated the idea of his product being used in a racist way, media pressure—ranging from local Bay Area newspapers to the national tech press—surely helped bring about such sweeping changes to the platform. That's because, like so many tech companies, Nextdoor doesn't make money—at least not yet. As a result, it's more beholden to investors than to the people who use the product. And while investors hate losing engagement, they hate headlines that tell the world the company they've funded is a home for racial profiling even more. Same with Facebook: the site walked back (though, of course, did not remove) its real-name policy only when a large contingent of users revolted and turned the story into a PR nightmare.

That's why we all need to pay a lot closer attention to the minutiae we encounter online—the form fields and menus we tend to gloss over so quickly. Because if we want tech companies to be more accountable, we need to be able to identify and articulate what's going wrong, and put pressure on them to change (or on government to regulate their actions).

It's never been more important that we demand this kind of accountability. Failing to design systems that reflect and represent diverse groups can alienate customers and make people feel marginalized on an individual level, and that would be reason enough for us to demand better. But there's also a pressing societal concern here. When systems don't allow users to express their identities, companies end up with data that doesn't reflect the reality of their users. And as we'll see in the coming chapters, when companies (and, increasingly, their artificial-intelligence systems) rely on that information to make choices about how their products work, they can wreak havoc—affecting everything from personal safety to political contests to prison sentences.

Chapter 5
Delighted to Death

One day in 2015, Dan Hon put his toddler, Calvin, on the scale. He was two and a half years old, and he clocked in at 29.2 pounds—up 1.9 pounds from the week before, and smack in the middle of the normal range for his age. Hon didn't think twice about it.

But his scale did. Later that week, Hon received Calvin's "Weekly Report" from Withings, the company that makes his "smart scale" and accompanying app. It told Calvin not to be discouraged about his weight gain, and to set a goal to "shed those extra pounds." [1]

"They even have his birth date in his profile," Hon tweeted about the incident. "But engagement still needs to send those notifications!" [2]

Withings specializes in "smart" scales, meaning internet-connected devices that save your data to an account you access using an app on your smartphone or other device. In the app, you can see your weight over time, track trends, and set goals.

An update from Dan Hon's "smart" scale, shaming his toddler son for gaining weight. (Dan Hon)

There's just one problem: the only goal Withings understands is weight loss.

Sometimes, like in Calvin's case, the result is comically absurd: most people would chuckle at the idea of a healthy two-year-old needing a weight goal. But in other cases, it might be downright hurtful. Like the default message that Withings sends if you weigh in at your lowest ever: "Congratulations! You've hit a new low weight!" the app exclaims. Hon's family got that one too—this time, for his wife. She'd just had a baby, not met a goal. But Withings can't tell the difference.

Have an eating disorder? Congratulations!

Just started chemo? Congratulations!

Chronically ill? Congratulations!

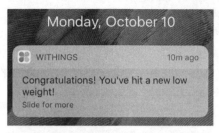

Withings is designed to congratulate any kind of weight loss—even if that's not your goal. (Dan Hon)

Withings is far from the only service with this problem. Everywhere you turn online, you'll find products that just can't wait to congratulate, motivate, and generally "engage" you . . . no matter what you think about it.

That's what went wrong in 2014 for Eric Meyer, whose tragic experience I described back in Chapter 1. Facebook wanted to delight its users, but instead it forced Meyer to relive the death of his daughter—putting her face in the center of his Year In Review, and surrounding her by illustrations of dancing party-goers and balloons.

As soon as Meyer and I began talking about this problem, people started sending us screenshots. So many screenshots, each more absurd than the last.

One of those came from Timehop, a service that "helps you celebrate the best moments of the past with your friends" [3] by re-sending you items that you posted to social media sites one or more years ago. This time, though, Timehop shared one of the worst moments from a user's past: when a man sent a message to his friends and family letting them know about where and when the memorial services for a young friend who had died suddenly would be held. According to Timehop, this wasn't a tragic memory; it was just "2010's longest Facebook post."[4]

Was that post really the right one to dredge back up? Probably not. But to make the situation much worse, Timehop also added its own canned commentary to the top of the notification:

THIS WAS A REALLY LONG POST THAT YOU WROTE IN
THE YEAR OF TWO THOUSAND AND WHATEVER[5]

It was meant to be funny, of course. But in this context, it comes off as condescending and judgmental—as if the user should have written less about his friend's death. Ouch.

In another example, a woman tried to email an airline a copy of her mother's death certificate. When she typed the word "death," the operating system, Apple iOS, kept suggesting that she add a cute little skull emoji to her message.

In yet another, Facebook turned all its reaction icons—the hearts, laughing faces, and the like that you can use to react to a friend's post—into spooky icons for Halloween. It was cute, unless you wanted to react to a serious post and all you had was a sad Frankenstein.

If you don't work in tech, you might be wondering at this point: What the hell are all these companies trying to *do*, exactly? Why do they care so much about shoving skulls and Frankensteins into our lives at awkward or sad moments? Why do they want us to relive funerals and tragedies? Why do we need to constantly be congratulated along the way?

Why won't our technology just leave us *alone*?

CELEBRATE THE WORST TIMES

On July 9, 2016, DeRay McKesson, one of the most prominent activists in the Black Lives Matter movement, was in Baton Rouge, Louisiana. He was there to protest the death of Alton Sterling, a thirty-seven-year-old black man who had been held down by police in front of a convenience store and shot at close range just a few days before.

McKesson—perhaps best known as @deray, the Twitter handle he uses to communicate with his several hundred thousand followers—had spent the day tweeting from the protests. He posted an image of a woman holding a home-made sign: "I can't keep calm. I have black sons," it read. He praised the community's efforts to de-escalate the situation with police. And he posted video of officers rushing up on protestors as they walked on the shoulder of a sidewalk-less highway.

McKesson was streaming the scene on Periscope, an app that broadcasts video directly to a live web feed, when police ran up behind him and placed him under arrest. He recorded the whole thing, including showing that he was staying well outside the painted line at the edge of the highway. He was charged with obstructing a highway of commerce anyway, and taken to jail with dozens of others.

McKesson had a long night in store for him. He would spend sixteen hours inside a cell, packed in like a sardine with as many as fifty other protestors.

It was also his thirty-first birthday.

I know this because, as I followed the news from Baton Rouge, I visited McKesson's Twitter feed. But rather than seeing

Twitter plastered DeRay McKesson's feed with balloons for his birthday—on the same night he was live-tweeting from a protest.

his latest tweets, I saw dozens of animated balloons flutter up my screen, obscuring his posts and videos.

The design was meant to be cute—to celebrate a user and remind followers of their birthday. But as I watched those multi-colored balloons twirl their way over pictures of police in riot gear and tweets fearing for people's safety, I was anything but charmed. It was dissonant, uncomfortable—a surreal reminder of just how distant designers and product managers can be from the realities of their users.

These sorts of misplaced celebrations are everywhere, from Dan Hon and his "smart" scale, to Eric Meyer and his Year In Review, to the everyday reminders to wish someone a happy birthday that we all get on Facebook. They would seem almost quaint, as if from a simpler time, back when social media was just fun and games—not the primary way people communicate with friends and family and engage with current events. Almost quaint, that is, if they didn't feel so unsettling.

WELCOME TO YOUR PAST

Another category where cute ideas turn creepy is reminders: features that are designed to encourage users to relive moments from their past, like we saw with Timehop. Timehop, at least, is specifically designed for this purpose: if you don't want to relive the past, you have no reason to sign up for it in the first place. But other digital products have no problem tacking on "hey, remember when" features, without your ever opting in.

The worst offender is Facebook, which never misses an opportunity to "reengage" its users. Year In Review was one of the first of these features, but in the last few years, we've seen tons more. The most widespread one is probably On This Day, which works basically just like Timehop—except that Facebook never asked if you wanted to use it. If you were on Facebook when it launched in 2015, you simply started receiving On This Day reminders—with no way to opt out. So perhaps it's no surprise that Facebook's help forums were filled with people begging for a way to turn off the feature, saying things like, "No one deserves to be reminded of things unwillingly" and "I NEVER WANTED THIS." They told stories of lost children, chronic disease, and divorce. Months later, Facebook finally allowed users to filter out specific people and dates—but On This Day couldn't simply be turned off. So frustrated users started sharing hacks they'd found to trick the feature. More than a year after the original launch, Facebook finally introduced the ability to turn off *notifications* from On This Day. But the application itself? It can't be deleted, no matter what you do.

Despite these problems, Facebook keeps expanding the feature. For example, it now also sends out Friendversary updates, which tell you that you became friends with a person on this date some number of years ago. Sometimes it's cute—until Facebook decides you need to relive your relationship with, say, an ex or an old boss.

In February 2016, on its twelfth anniversary, Facebook took this concept even further and created a fake holiday called Friends Day. To celebrate, it built minute-long videos for every user. Each video was constructed from photos plucked from the user's account, with the goal of highlighting all the good times they'd had with their friends.

Only, human editors weren't creating these videos, of course—not for more than a billion users. The photos were algorithmically selected, and as usual, the algorithm didn't always get it right. "Hi Tyler," one man's video starts, using title cards. "Here are your friends." He's then shown five copies of the same photo. The result is equal parts funny and sad—like he has just that one friend. It only gets better (or worse, depending on your sense of humor) from there. Another title card comes up: "You've done a lot together," followed by a series of photos of wrecked vehicles, culminating in a photo of an injured man giving the thumbs up from a hospital bed. I suppose Facebook isn't wrong, exactly: getting in a car accident is one definition of "doing a lot together."

The video keeps going. "You've shared these moments," it says. Then the same photos display again, like we're all stuck in some kind of tragicomic loop. By the 37-second mark, I'm absolutely losing it: a title card comes up, saying, "And remember this?"—and then displays one of the wrecked vehicles for the third time. After one last repeat of the hospital bed photo (title card: "Your friends are pretty awesome"), the video wraps with a hearty "Happy Friends Day" message from Facebook. And, of course, it's all set to the kind of peppy tune you'd expect when you're waiting for a conference call to start.

Then there's Facebook Moments, which launched in the summer of 2016. This feature allows you to do things like create collections of photos taken by multiple people at a single event. But like the Friends Day video, Moments also automatically creates montages, and sets them to music. You can probably guess what went wrong: in one, Facebook created a montage of a man's near-fatal car crash, set to an acoustic-jazz ditty. Just imagine your photos of a totaled car and scraped-up arms, taken on a day you thought you might die, set to a soft scat vocal track. *Doo-be-doo-duh-duh*, indeed.

It's not just Facebook either. Google Photos launched a similar feature in 2016—resulting in a baby's Catholic baptism video being automatically set to cheesy techno music.

These videos are truly absurd—seriously, take a break right now and go watch them.[6] And then consider this: Why are tech companies so determined to take your content out of its original context and serve it up to you in a tidy, branded package?

NEVER MISS A TERRIBLE THING

One day in September 2016, Sally Rooney felt her phone buzz. She looked at the screen and saw a notification from Tumblr: "Beep beep! #neo-nazis is here!" it read.

Rooney's not a neo-Nazi. She's an Irish novelist. "I just

Sally Rooney's Tumblr
notification. (Sally Rooney)

downloaded the app—I didn't change any of the original settings, and I wasn't following that tag or indeed any tags," she told me. "I had a moment of paranoia wondering if I'd accidentally followed #neo-nazis, but I hadn't." [7]

Yet there Rooney was anyway, getting alerts about neo-Nazis, wrapped up in the sort of cutesy, childish little package you'd expect to hear in a preschool. How did this happen? After a screenshot of the notification went viral on Twitter, a Tumblr employee told Rooney that it was probably a "what you missed" notification. Rooney had previously read posts about the rise in fascism, and the notification system had used her past behavior to predict that she might be interested in more neo-Nazi content.

Now on to the copy. As you might guess, no one at Tumblr sat down and wrote that terrible sentence. They wrote a *text string*: a piece of canned copy into which any topic could be inserted automatically: "Beep beep! #[trending tag] is here!" (In fact, another Tumblr user shared a version of the notification he received: "Beep beep! #mental-illness is here!")

Text strings like these are used all the time in software to tailor a message to its context—like when I log into my bank account and it says, "Hello, Sara" at the top. But in the last few years, tech companies have become obsessed with bringing more "personality" into their products, and this kind of copy is often the first place they do it—making it cute, quirky, and "fun." I'll even take a little blame for this. In my work as a content strategy consultant, I've helped lots of organizations develop a voice for their online content, and encouraged them to make their writing more human and conversational. If only I'd known that we would end up with so many inappropriate, trying-too-hard, chatty tech products.

One of those products is Medium, the online-publishing platform launched in 2012 by Ev Williams, one of Twitter's original founders. In the spring of 2015, Kevin M. Hoffman wrote a post on Medium about his friend Elizabeth, who had recently died of cancer. Hoffman works in tech, in web design and information architecture, and he knew Elizabeth from their time spent putting on conferences together. So he wanted to share his memorial in a place his peers, and hers, would see it. Medium was an obvious choice.

A few hours after posting his memorial, he got an email from Medium letting him know how his post was doing, and telling him that three people had recommended it. And inserted in that email was the headline he had written for his post, "In Remembrance of Elizabeth," followed by a string of copy: "Fun fact: Shakespeare only got 2 recommends on his first Medium story."

It's meant to be humorous—a light, cheery joke, a bit of throw-away text to brighten your day. If you're not grieving a friend, that is. Or writing about a tragedy, or a job loss, or, I don't know, systemic racial inequalities in the US criminal justice system. All of which are topics that you might find on Medium, a site that mixes paid journalistic pieces with free, anyone-can-be-an-author posts.

When the design and product team at Medium saw Kevin's screenshot, they cringed too—and immediately went through their copy strings, removing the ones that might feel insensitive or inappropriate in some contexts. Because, it turns out, one of the key components of having a great personality is knowing when to express it, and when to hold back. That's a skill most humans learn as they grow up and navigate social situations—but, sadly, seem to forget as soon as they're tasked with making a dumb machine "sound human."

That's why I find Siri, Apple's virtual assistant, so grating. As we learned in Chapter 1, when Siri doesn't understand, or thinks you're messing with it, it teases you. It's marginally funny—if you'd rather get sass back from your phone than have it simply try to help. ("Hey Siri, what should I get my mom for Christmas?" "I hear the internet is good for these kinds of questions." Sick burn, I guess . . . but wouldn't most people rather that the assistant just looked up the phrase "Christmas gifts for moms" instead?) Maybe I'm the only one who's just not interested in snotty comebacks from my phone, though I doubt it. But even if it works sometimes—even if it makes some people laugh uproariously—it's hard to imagine anything less helpful during a crisis than a robot voice parroting canned humor at me.

The problem is that Siri just doesn't know the difference—

because for all its artificial intelligence, its emotional intelligence is basically nonexistent. And that's fine, actually. Siri's not a person; it's a virtual assistant that can't speak without adding awkward pauses at every comma. Why should it be good at navigating the complexity of human experience? It's that it tries too hard to slather a thin layer of personality on top of a system that's nowhere near socially advanced enough for wit—and the result feels a little like someone interrupting a funeral with a fart joke.

That's something the team at email marketing platform MailChimp learned firsthand (well, the part about personality being tricky to get right, at least; I don't know what they think about fart jokes). A few years back, MailChimp invested tons of time in building a voice for its brand—from its jovial mascot, Freddie the chimp, to its commitment to writing legal terms and conditions in plain English. In 2011, the company published these guidelines on a public website, Voice & Tone (voiceandtone.com)—and soon, those guidelines were featured on *Fast Company* and popping up in countless conference talks as the way forward for online communication. You could almost say they ushered in the talk-like-a-human movement in tech products. So, in the summer of 2015, when Eric Meyer and I were researching empathetic web content and design practices, we called up MailChimp's communications director, Kate Kiefer Lee. And what she told us surprised me: MailChimp was, slowly but surely, pulling back from its punchy, jokey voice. When I asked what had gone wrong, Kiefer Lee told me there were too many things to count.

In one instance, the team was brainstorming ideas for a 404 page. On the web, a 404 error means "page not found," so a 404 page is where you're redirected if you try to click a broken link.

They usually say something like, "The page you are looking for does not exist." But at the time, the team was really focused on developing a funny, unique voice for MailChimp. So they decided to call it an "oops" moment and started brainstorming funny ways to communicate that idea. Pretty soon, someone had designed a page showing a pregnancy test with a positive sign. Everyone thought this was hilarious—right up until Kiefer Lee took it to her CEO. "Absolutely not," he told her. Looking back, she's glad he killed it. "We wanted to be funny and delight people. I think we were trying too hard to be entertaining." [8]

Realizations like this made Kiefer Lee and her team turn a more critical eye to the way MailChimp was communicating— particularly around touchy subjects, like someone being banned from the service for sending spam, or a user's credit card being declined. "We focus on clarity over cleverness and personality," she told me. "We are not in an industry that is associated with crisis, but we don't know what our readers and customers are going through. And our readers and customers are people. They could be in an emergency and they still have to use the internet." [9]

Other tech companies haven't caught up. In fact, in recent years, I'd argue, the trend has gotten worse, morphing into some truly awful design choices along the way.

THE SHAME GAME

You know when you try to shop online or read an article, but a little window pops up before you can even see what you're looking at, trying to get you to sign up for the site's email list? I'm sure you do, because you can barely use the internet without this happening. In tech, we call these kinds of pop-ups *opt-ins*, meaning you're being asked to choose to receive marketing messages from a company. If you click the "no thanks" option, that's an *opt-out*. But not only is the design intrusive and frustrating—*Can I at least see your products before being badgered into daily emails?*—there's a new design trend that's making them even worse: rather than tapping a button that says "no thanks," sites are now making users click condescending, passive-aggressive statements to get the intrusive window to close:

> No thanks, I hate saving money.
> No thanks, this deal is just too good for me.
> I'm not interested in being awesome.
> I'd rather stay uninformed.

Ew, right? Do you want to do business with a company that talks to you this way?

I guess you could say these blamey, shamey messages are more "human" than a simple yes/no—but only if the human you're imagining is the jerkiest jerk you ever dated, the kind of person who was happy to hurt your feelings and kill your self-esteem to get their way. That's why I started calling these opt-in offers "marketing negging."

Negging, if you're lucky enough to be unfamiliar, is a technique used by the "pickup artist" (PUA) community—a loose association of men who share tricks and manipulation tactics designed to help them pick up as many women as possible. The term comes from an abbreviation of "negative," and the concept is simple: you walk up to a woman and use subtle digs and passive-aggressive faux compliments to "lower a girl's social value in relation to yours," as the popular PUA site Seduction Science puts it.[10] The idea is to erode a woman's self-esteem and make her feel like she can't do any better. Maybe you tell her that her roots are showing. Maybe you tell her that she's too pretty to wear such an unflattering outfit. Then, the theory goes, she'll feel vulnerable, and be more likely to say yes to you. PUA websites (of which there are many, and which I cannot, in good conscience, suggest you visit) are littered with lines like these, and many of the men who use these forums obsessively test them out, reporting back on what works and what doesn't.

Negging is creepy as hell, treating women as objects to be collected at all costs. These shamey opt-out messages do pretty much the same thing to all of us online: they manipulate our emotions so that companies can collect our information, without actually doing any of the work of creating a relationship or building a loyal following. And, just like the men who frequent PUA forums and make spreadsheets of which pickup lines work most often, companies spend endless hours testing out different copy strings, and analyzing which ones are most effective.

These sorts of jokingly nasty messages might seem like the polar opposite of the friendly, overly celebratory ones we've looked at so far in this chapter. But I would argue they're not so different at all. What they all do is wrap tech's real motives—gaining access to more information, making us more dependent on their services—in a cloak of cuteness that gently conditions us to go along with whatever's been plunked down in front of us. *There, there, dear. Don't worry about what we're doing with your account. Have a balloon.* And if we're not on board—if we don't acquiesce to their negging or laugh at their jokes or reminisce when they want us to—then we're just no fun.

BLINDED BY DELIGHT

It was the spring of 2012, and I was sitting at a glass conference table in a glassed-in conference room in a fancy building high above Manhattan's West Side Highway, brainstorming ideas for redesigning a major bank's credit card rewards program. The brief we were given at the start of the session: come up with fun, unexpected ways to curate and customize the offers that card-holders receive—you know, get double points for shopping at the Gap this month, or whatever.

"What if we customized offers based on the weather!?" an account planner said.

"Ooh, what about filtering offers based on your *horoscope*?" a designer suggested.

"But no matter what, it needs to be delightful—more like Pinterest!" the creative director insisted.

I looked around the room, bewildered. Why would anyone *want* their credit card offers to be dependent on the weather? What, precisely, would we do to make a 1-800-Flowers purchase particularly relevant to a Scorpio? And who would think that just because people might enjoy idly skimming haircut ideas or DIY craft projects on Pinterest, they also want to spend hours scrolling through endless "limited-time offers"?

I didn't say any of that, of course. I didn't say much at all. Mostly, I wondered to myself, "How the hell did I end up here?"

That part's easy: a few months earlier, I'd quit my seventy-hour-a-week job at an agency to start my own consulting busi-ness. I was twenty-eight and scared as hell. I was also working on my first book (which I was certain I had no business writing) and planning a cross-country move (from a place I hated to a place I was sure I'd also dislike). My life felt like one big risky venture. So when an agency in New York contacted me, saying they needed a content strategist for a large project, I jumped at the opportunity—mostly because it meant not worrying about finding clients for a few months.

So there I was, trying as best I could to advocate for the people we were supposed to be designing for: cardholders who wanted to understand how to get the most value out of their credit cards. But time and again, the conversation turned away from how to make the program useful, and toward that word I find so empty: "delight."

Delight is a concept that's been tossed around endlessly in the tech industry these past few years, and I've always hated it. "Is there a formula for delight?" one article on a design website asks (um, no, there isn't). "When a product is delightful, it just makes sense," starts another (or, maybe more likely, in order for a product to ever be considered delightful, it first has to make sense). "Take your user experience to the next level by adding delight!" exhorts yet another (what, is delight an ice cream topping now?).

And that's the sort of design sensibility we've seen throughout this chapter: clever copy, peppy music, the insistence that your memories must be rehashed and shared. All of it is based on the belief that true delight can be reduced to the digital equivalent of whipped cream in a can: a layer of fluffy sweetness sprayed on top of the experience. But as we've seen over and over, when teams laser-focus on delight, they lose sight of all the ways that fun and quirky design can fail—creating experiences that are dissonant, painful, or inappropriate.

Humans are notoriously bad at noticing one thing when

we've been primed to look for something else instead. There's even a term for it: "inattentional blindness." Coined by research psychologists Arien Mack and Irvin Rock back in the 1990s,[11] *inattentional blindness* is a phenomenon in which humans fail to perceive major things happening in front of their eyes when their attention has been focused on something else.

The most famous demonstration of inattentional blindness in action is known as the "invisible gorilla" test, in which participants watch a video of two groups of basketball players, one wearing white shirts and the other wearing black shirts. Before watching, they're asked to count how many times a player wearing a white shirt passes the ball. Halfway through the one-minute video, a person in a gorilla suit walks into the scene and beats their chest, staying on-screen for a total of nine seconds. Half the participants routinely fail to notice the gorilla.[12]

This study has been replicated and tweaked lots of times, and the results are more or less the same: when people focus on one task, their attention narrows, dramatically decreasing the likelihood that they'll notice other details. In fact, more recently, researchers tried a similar experiment with radiologists—a group highly trained to look closely at information and identify abnormalities. In this experiment, a gorilla the size of a matchbook was superimposed onto scans of lungs. The radiologists were then asked to look for signs of cancer on the scans. A full 83 percent of them failed to notice the gorilla.[13]

Designers, like radiologists, pride themselves on attention to detail: they obsess over typographic elements like line kerning and spacing; they spend hours debating between nearly identical colors; they notice immediately when an object is a few pixels off center. Of course they do; those are the sorts of things they've been trained to notice. They'd be laughed out of design school and off the internet otherwise. But if they've never been asked to notice how their work might fail people—or been made rudely aware of the problem after it has—they're just as blind as the rest of us. So when a design brief says to focus on new ways to delight and engage users, their brains turn immediately toward the positive: vacation photos flitting by to a jazzy beat, birthday balloons floating up a happy Twitter timeline. In this idealized universe, we all keep beep-beeping along, no neo-Nazis in sight.

In *Design for Real Life*, Eric Meyer and I urged designers to combat this kind of blindness by building in steps that force them to question how and when their fun-and-friendly features could fail. After all, most designers aren't out there aiming to harm their users, and taking a moment to identify stress cases and find fractures in their work would ferret out a lot of problems. But these sorts of gentle nudges aren't enough in a tech culture where "user engagement" trumps all—where it's more important to gather user data and inflate valuation numbers before an acquisition than it is to care for the actual people affected by a design choice.

Take any one of the examples in this chapter, and just underneath its feel-good veneer you'll find a business goal that might not make you smile. For example, Twitter's birthday balloons are designed to encourage people to send good wishes to one another. They're positioned as harmless fun: a little dose of delight that makes users feel more engaged with Twitter. But of course, Twitter doesn't really care about celebrating your special day. It cares about gathering your birth date, so that your user profile is more valuable to advertisers. The fluttering balloons are an enticement, not a feature. Delight, in this case, is a distraction—a set of blinders that make it easy for designers to miss all the contexts in which birthday balloons are inappropriate, while conveniently glossing over the reason Twitter is gathering data in the first place.

The same is true for all those Facebook features designed to make you relive your past. Facebook has an internal metric that it uses alongside the typical DAUs (daily active users) and MAUs (monthly active users). It calls this metric CAUs, for "cares about us." CAUs gauge precisely what they sound like: how much users believe that Facebook cares about them. Tech-industry insider publication *The Information* reported in early 2016 that nudging CAUs upward had become an obsession for Facebook leadership.[14]

But the metric doesn't gauge whether Facebook *actually* cares about users. All that matters is whether you *feel* like it does. Warm-and-fuzzy features like On This Day, which sends reminders about past posts, and Moments, which creates those peppy video collages, are aimed squarely at making you feel like Facebook cares about you on a personal level. And as long as that's happening on the surface, Facebook is free to keep dealing in user data in ever-more-worrisome ways, including not just tracking what you say and do on its site, but also buying up dossiers on users from third-party data brokers (something we'll look at more closely in the next chapter).

Or consider those ridiculous email sign-up forms with their icky opt-out messages. It would be almost refreshing if companies wanted to gather your email address only so that they could send you more spam. But there's a more insidious goal here too: companies that are seeking to be acquired (which is what a good percentage of tech startups want) are valued higher when they have larger subscriber lists.[15] Personal data, in this case, is an asset in and of itself—even if the quality of the list is low. That's why these companies are so shameless: They're not really trying to build loyalty. All they want is data.

FAKE FRIENDS

The neo-Nazi Tumblr notification that Sally Rooney received struck a nerve: as I write this, her screenshot has been retweeted nearly seven thousand times, and "liked" more than twelve thousand times—a pretty big feat, considering that most tweets die out within a few minutes of being posted. It even caught the attention of Tumblr's head writer, Tag Savage. "We talked about getting rid of it but it performs kinda great,"[16] he wrote on Twitter, as Rooney's screenshot went viral.

When Savage says the "beep beep!" message "performs," he means that the notification gets a lot of people to open up Tumblr—a boon for a company invested in DAUs and MAUs. And for most tech companies, that's all that matters. Questions like, "is it ethical?" or "is it appropriate?" simply aren't part of the equation, because ROI always wins out.

All these cutesy copy strings and celebratory features create a false intimacy between us and the products we use. We're not actually friends with our digital products, no matter how great their personalities might seem at first. Real friends don't create metrics to gauge whether people *think* they care. They don't try to tell you jokes when you're in the middle of a crisis. They don't force you to relive trauma, or write off hate speech, or any of the things tech products routinely do in the name of engagement. They simply care. Tech companies, on the other hand, use "personality" to manipulate us—to keep us clicking and tapping and liking and reading and saving and faving, while, just outside the screen, they flout regulations, steal data, and keep oppressive systems intact. It's time we see through them.

Chapter 6

Tracked, Tagged, and Targeted

It was December 2016, and I was sitting in the back of a blindingly white room on Mulberry Street in Manhattan's Nolita neighborhood, next door to a clothing boutique and a place selling French tartines and overpriced salads. It looked like an Apple Store crossed with an art gallery—just the kind of pricey pop-up shop you'd expect to see in this upscale downtown neighborhood two weeks before Christmas. Black-and-white photos lined the walls. Shiny tablets beckoned from gleaming-white tables. A security guard stood at the door. Perched next to me on a row of tall, white stools was a series of customers, coats and shopping bags in hand, waiting for assistance from one of the many staffers clad all in white.

It *looked* like an Apple Store, until you saw what was happening on all those screens. On one tablet, a video told the story of data brokers: the companies that make their millions mashing up data about you from as many online and offline sources as possible, and selling it to countless companies. Another displayed data from a "predictive policing" software program designed for law enforcement. The software combines historical crime data with a host of other factors—the weather, locations of bars, and even analysis of social media posts—to determine where and when crimes might occur. Yet another demonstrated how much could be learned about a person from just their email's metadata (which is what the NSA was collecting until 2011): subject line, sender, recipient, time stamp, and the like. The answer? Often, enough to pinpoint where a person was and what they were doing at any given time.

As you've likely guessed, this wasn't a store at all. This was the Glass Room: an immersive installation that encouraged visitors to "consider how you use technology and how those behind technology use you." Curated by the nonprofit Tactical Technology Collective and funded by Mozilla, makers of the Firefox internet browser, the Glass Room painted a bleak picture of just how much personal information can be gleaned from our daily technology use—from the links we click to the posts we like to the real-life places we go while our phones are simply sitting in our pockets—and how that data gets transformed from individual strings into massive tomes.

Half the people in the room were there on purpose, like me—tech enthusiasts, privacy advocates, civil servants working on open-data initiatives. The other half had simply wandered in on a cold Friday evening, and found themselves interested enough to stay. That's who was sitting next to me in the back of the room, listening to the staff explain how to disentangle your online identity from all those trackers and data brokers.

Before I left, I was handed a "Data Detox Kit": a thick envelope stuffed with eight days' worth of activities designed to help people see how they're being tracked, and change both their security settings and their technology habits to minimize it in the future. On the train home, I cracked open the kit. Day one was "discovery": clearing out browser cookies, that sort of thing. I moved on to day two: "being social."

"Is Facebook your BFF?" the headline asked. The kit prompted me to find out by downloading a browser extension: What Facebook Thinks You Like. The extension trawls Facebook's ad-serving settings, and spits out a list of keywords the site thinks you're interested in, and why. There's the expected stuff: travel, lipstick, Danish design. I've probably clicked on ads for those things before. Then there's a host of just plain bizarre connections: "Neighbors (1981 Film)," a film I've never seen and don't know anything about. A host of no-context nouns: "Girlfriend," "Brand," "Wall," "Extended essay," "Eternity." I have no idea where any of this comes from—or what sort of advertising it would make me a target for. Then it gets creepy: "returned from trip 1 week ago," "frequent international travelers." I rarely post anything to Facebook, but it knows where I go, and how often.

As of December 2016, ProPublica—the nonprofit news organization that made the What Facebook Thinks You Like browser extension—said its project had collected 52,000 unique attributes like these. But it also revealed something else: while Facebook will show you what it has inferred about you from your activity on the site, it won't show you all the other information it has about you—information purchased from third-party data brokers.[1] That additional data set might include all sorts of things: where you shop (from loyalty card usage), whether you own a car or a home (public records), which publications you get (subscriber lists).

In 2012, one of the largest of these brokers, Acxiom, bragged that it had an average of 1,500 data points for each of the 500 million consumers, including most of the adult population in the United States, in its database.[2] Think about that: 1,500 individual tidbits of information about you, all stored in a database somewhere and handed out to whoever will pay the price. Then there's the practice of segmenting: grouping you into one of Acxiom's seventy marketing clusters, each with a branded name and a peppy description.

Judging by the information readily available about me, I'm almost certain Acxiom's database has me pegged as a segment 6, "Casual Comfort": a city-living, upwardly mobile type who enjoys "socializing, attending concerts and participating in fantasy sports leagues, as well as adventurous outdoor recreation. This cluster also appreciates fine dining and fitness."[3] Minus the fantasy sports, this is all pretty accurate. And why wouldn't it be? After all, Acxiom knows which credit cards I have, how much I paid for my house, and where I spend my money. When this data is assembled into a dossier and matched up with my Facebook habits, boom: you get a detailed view of not just how much I make and what I like to do, but also where I am at almost any given moment, what I believe in and care about, and who my friends are.

Data collection may be creepy, but it's certainly not just tech companies that are doing it: everyone from your grocery store to your bank to your insurance company is neck-deep in detailed information about you and your habits. In many ways, this is simply our modern reality, particularly in the United States, where regulations are piecemeal. It's a reality that we'd be smart to acknowledge, if we hope to stop its abuses or regulate its effects.[4] But while our digital products aren't solely to blame, they do enable this data collection—and maybe more important, they normalize it in our daily lives.

As we'll see in this chapter, every bit of the design process—from the default settings we talked about in Chapter 3, to the form fields in Chapter 4, to the cute features and clever copy in Chapter 5—creates an environment where we're patronized, pushed, and misled into providing data; where the data collected is often incorrect or based on assumptions; and where it's almost impossible for us to understand what's being done by whom.

DEFAULTING TO DECEPTION

In November of 2016, ride-hailing company Uber released a new update to its iPhone app—and with it, a new detail you might have glossed right over while you were tapping "accept" and "continue": rather than tracking your location while you're using the app (which makes sense, since GPS location helps your driver find you easily), Uber now defaults to tracking your location all the time, even when the app is closed. Did that make your eyes widen? It should: this means that if you're an iPhone user and an Uber customer, you've probably given Uber permission to track you wherever you go, whenever the company wants.

Uber promises it won't do anything malevolent, of course. The company says its new data collection practices are all about improving service (which is the stock PR line). In this case, Uber says the changes are designed to make pickups and drop-offs safer and easier. For example, the company says it wants to know how often riders cross the street directly after leaving their driver's vehicle, which it thinks could indicate that drivers are dropping passengers off in unsafe locations. Uber also wants to do a better job of tracking people's locations while they're waiting for their car to arrive, because the top reason drivers and customers contact each other before pickup is to confirm precise location. To do all this, Uber says it wants to use a rider's location only from the moment they request a car until five minutes after they've been dropped off—not all the time. Phew, right?

But iPhone settings don't actually work that way. There are only three options: you can allow an app to use your location at all times, only while you're using the app, or never. This Uber update purposely disables the middle option, so all you're left with are the extremes. And while you *can* select "never," Uber strongly discourages it, even misleading you along the way: doing so triggers a pop-up in the app with a large headline, "Uber needs your location to continue," followed by a big button that says "enable location services." By all appearances, you don't have a choice: Uber *needs* it, after all. But just below that, if you're paying close attention (something I'm sure we all do when we're tapping through screens, right? Right?), you'll see a much smaller text link: "enter pickup address." That little link bypasses the location-based option, and instead allows you to just type in the street address where you want to be picked up. Because, it turns out, you certainly *can* use Uber without location data. The company just doesn't want you to.

When we look at these choices together, a clear picture emerges: Uber designed its application to default to the most permissive data collection settings. It disabled the option that would have allowed customers to use the app in the most convenient way, while still retaining some control over how much of their data Uber has permission to access. And it created a screen that is designed expressly to deceive you into thinking you *have* to allow Uber to track your location in order to use the service, even though that's not true. The result is a false dichotomy: all or nothing, in or out. But that's the thing about defaults: they're designed to achieve a desired outcome. Just not yours.

Uber claims it's not out to track your every move; it only wants just a bit more data after your ride is over. Should we take the company at its word? No, one anonymous user told tech publication the *Verge*: "I simply don't trust Uber to limit their location tracking to 'five minutes after the trip ends.' There's nothing I can do to enforce this as an end user." [5]

That's true: Apple's settings just say "always." And while Uber might not be doing anything else with our data today, I'm not sure the "just trust us" approach is a great long-term plan when you're talking about aggressively growing startups backed by millions in venture capital—money they'll need to show investors that they can recoup in the not-too-distant future. Particularly when we're talking about Uber—a company with a truly abysmal privacy record.

In 2014, an executive used the software's "god view"—which shows customers' real-time movements, as well as their ride history—to track a journalist who was critical of the company. Other sources have claimed that most corporate employees have unfettered access to customers' ride data—and have, at times, tracked individual users just for fun. [6] In 2012, Uber even published an official blog post bragging about how it can tell when users have had a one-night stand—dubbing them, somewhat grossly, "rides of glory." (Uber deleted the post a couple years later, when major stories started breaking about its disregard for privacy.)[7] All said, Uber is well known for having a male-dominated workplace that sees no problem playing fast and loose with ethics (a problem we'll look at more closely in Chapter 9). And as we've seen, that culture has made its way right into the default design of its app.

Default settings—particularly those in the apps on our always-with-us smartphones—not only encode bias, as we saw earlier. They also play a massive role in the data that can be collected about us. And often we don't even notice it's happening, because each little screen is designed to encourage us along: *yes, I agree, continue.* Tap, tap, tap. It all feels simple, inevitable almost—until you open your phone's settings and realize that dozens of apps are quietly collecting your location data.

Back in 2010, technologist Tim Jones, then of the Electronic Frontier Foundation, wrote that he had asked his Twitter followers to help him come up with a name for this method of using "deliberately confusing jargon and user-interfaces" to "trick your users into sharing more info about themselves than they really want to."[8] One of the most popular suggestions was *Zuckering.* The term, of course, refers to Mark Zuckerberg, Facebook's founder—who, a few months before, had dramatically altered Facebook's default privacy settings. Facebook insisted that the changes were empowering—that its new features would give the 350 million users it had at the time the tools to "personalize their privacy,"[9] by offering more granular controls over who can see what.

The way Facebook implemented this change isn't quite as inspirational, though. During the transition, users were given only two options: if they had customized their settings in the past, they could preserve them; otherwise, they would default to a "recommended" setting from Facebook. Only, the new default settings weren't anything like the old ones. In the past, profile information like gender and relationship status was visible to friends only by default. The new settings made that information public. Perhaps even more worrisome, anything you posted to Facebook, which had previously been viewable by "Your Networks and Friends" only, was also made public. None of this was explained in the transition tool either; it was instead presented as a simple default choice—just click yes and be done with it. Finding out what you were really agreeing to took extra clicks out of the transition tool, and into Facebook's complicated privacy settings page. Because, ultimately, Facebook didn't want you to actually customize your settings. It wanted to Zucker you out of as much data as possible.

As I write this, seven years later, nothing has changed—except that as mobile usage has skyrocketed, the amount of data that can be harvested from us has exploded. And companies like Uber? They're taking Zuckering further than ever.

APPROXIMATING YOU

Back in 2012, Google thought I was a man.

Let me back up. Back in January of that year, the search giant released a new privacy policy that, for the first time, sought to aggregate your usage data from across its array of products—including Google Search, Gmail, Google Calendar, YouTube, and others—into a single profile.[10] This change caused quite a stir, both inside and outside of tech circles, and as a result, users flocked to the "ad preferences" section of their profiles, where

Google had listed the categories that a user seemed to be interested in, as inferred from their web usage patterns—like "Computers & Electronics," or "Parenting." But in addition to those categories, Google listed the age range and gender it thought you were. It thought I was a man, and somewhere between thirty-five and forty-four. I was twenty-eight.

Pretty soon, I realized it wasn't just me: Tons of the women in my professional circle were buzzing about it on Twitter—all labeled as men. So were female writers at *Mashable*, a tech media site; the *Mary Sue*, which covers geek pop culture from a feminist perspective; and *Forbes*, the business magazine. So, what did all of us have in common? Our search histories were littered with topics like web development, finance, and sci-fi. In other words, we searched like men. Or at least, that's what Google thought.[11]

What Google was doing is something that's now commonplace for tech products: it was using *proxies*. A proxy is a stand-in for real knowledge—similar to the personas that designers use as a stand-in for their real audience. But in this case, we're talking about proxy data: when you don't have a piece of information about a user that you want, you use data you *do* have to infer that information. Here, Google wanted to track my age and gender, because advertisers place a high value on this information. But since Google didn't have demographic data at the time, it tried to infer those facts from something it had lots of: my behavioral data.

The problem with this kind of proxy, though, is that it relies on assumptions—and those assumptions get embedded more deeply over time. So if your model assumes, from what it has seen and heard in the past, that most people interested in technology are men, it will learn to code users who visit tech websites as more likely to be male. Once that assumption is baked in, it skews the results: the more often women are incorrectly labeled as men, the more it looks like men dominate tech websites—and the more strongly the system starts to correlate tech website usage with men.

In short, proxy data can actually make a system *less* accurate over time, not more, without you even realizing it. Yet much of the data stored about us is proxy data, from ZIP codes being used to predict creditworthiness, to SAT scores being used to predict teens' driving habits.

It's easy to say it doesn't really matter that Google often gets gender wrong; after all, it's just going to use that information to serve up more "relevant" advertising. If most of us would rather ignore advertising anyway, who cares? But consider the potential ramifications: if, for example, Google frequently coded women who worked in technology in 2012 as men, then it could have skewed data about the readership of tech publications to look more male than it actually was. People who run media sites pay close attention to their audience data, and use it to make decisions. If they believed their audiences were more male than they were, they might think, "Well, maybe women *do* just care less about technology"—an argument they've no doubt heard before. That might skew publications' reporting on the gender gap in tech companies to focus more on the "pipeline," and less on structural and cultural problems that keep women out. After all, if women interested in technology don't exist, how could employers hire them?

This is theoretical, sure: I don't know how often Google got gender wrong back then, and I don't know how much that affected the way the tech industry continued to be perceived. But that's the problem: neither does Google. Proxies are naturally inexact, writes data scientist Cathy O'Neil in *Weapons of Math Destruction*. Even worse, they're self-perpetuating: they "define their own reality and use it to justify their results."[12]

Now, Google doesn't think I'm a man anymore. Sometime in the last five years, it sorted that out (not surprising, since Google now knows a lot more about me, including how often I shop for dresses and search for haircut ideas). But that doesn't stop other tech companies from relying on proxies—including Facebook. In the fall of 2016, journalists at *ProPublica* found that Facebook was allowing advertisers to target customers according to their race, even when they were advertising housing—something that's been blatantly illegal since the federal Fair Housing Act of 1968. To test the system, *ProPublica* posted an ad with a $50 budget, and chose to target users who were tagged as "likely to move" or as having an interest in topics like "buying a house" (some of those zillions of attributes we talked about earlier), while excluding users who were African American, Asian American, and Hispanic. The ad was approved right away. Then they showed the result to civil rights lawyer John Relman. He gasped. "This is horrifying," he told them. "This is massively illegal."[13]

But hold up: Facebook doesn't actually let us put our race on our profile. So how can it allow advertisers to segment that way? By proxies, of course. See, what Facebook offers advertisers isn't *really* the ability to target by race and ethnicity. It targets by ethnic *affinity*. In other words, if you've liked posts or pages that, according to Facebook's algorithm, suggest you're interested in content about a particular racial or ethnic group, then you might be included. Except Facebook didn't really position it that way for advertisers: when *ProPublica* created its ad, Facebook had placed the ethnic-affinity menu in the "demographics" section—a crystal-clear sign that this selection wasn't just about interests, but about identity.

There are legitimate reasons for Facebook to offer ethnicity-based targeting—for example, so that a hair product designed for black women is actually targeted at black women, or so that a Hispanic community group reaches Hispanic people. That makes sense. And since *ProPublica*'s report, Facebook has started excluding certain types of ads, such as those for housing, credit, and employment, from using ethnic-affinity targeting. But by using proxy data, Facebook didn't just open the door for discriminatory ads; it also opened a potential legal loophole: they can deny that they were operating illegally, because they weren't filtering users by race, but only by *interest* in race-related content. *Sure.*

There's also something deeply worrisome about Facebook assigning users an identity on the back end, while not allowing those same users to select their own identity in the front end of the system, says Safiya Noble, the information studies scholar we heard from back in Chapter 1. "We are being racially profiled by a platform that doesn't allow us to even declare our own race and ethnicity," she told me. "What does that mean to not allow culture and ethnicity to be visible in the platform?" [14]

What it means is that Facebook, once again, controls how its users represent themselves online—preventing people from choosing to identify themselves the way they'd like, while enabling advertisers to make assumptions. And because all this is happening via proxy data, it's obscured from view—so most of us never even realize it's happening.

PRODUCT KNOWS BEST

In the previous chapter I talked about how the endless barrage of cutesy copy and playful design features creates a false intimacy between us and our digital products—a fake friendship built by tech companies to keep us happily tapping out messages and hitting "like," no matter what they're doing behind the curtain. Writer Jesse Barron calls this "cuteness applied in the service of power-concealment":[15] an effort, on the part of tech companies, to make you feel safe and comfortable using their products, while they quietly hold the upper hand.

According to Barron, tech products do this by employing "caretaker speech"—the linguistics term used to describe the way we talk to children. For example, when Seamless, a popular food delivery app, sends cutesy emails about the status of his order, he writes, "I picture a cool babysitter, Skylar, with his jean vest, telling me as he microwaves a pop-tart that 'deliciousness is in the works,' his tone just grazing the surface of mockery." [16]

But no matter how cool the babysitter—no matter how far past bedtime Skylar lets us stay up—at the end of the evening we're still kids under someone else's control. The result is an environment where we start to accept that the tech products we use, and the companies behind them, know best—and we're just along for the ride.

In this way, cuteness becomes another cloak for tech companies: a shiny object that deflects criticism. Because the more we focus on the balloons and streamers, the clever videos and animated icons and punny humor, the less we'll question why companies are asking us for so much information. The less we'll notice just how much of our identities Facebook is making assumptions about, and who's using those assumptions for their own purposes. The less we'll care that almost every app we use is investing thousands of hours into figuring out new ways to squeeze information out of our usage patterns.

All this paternalistic playfulness, in other words, makes us childlike: just a bunch of kids refreshing screens and tapping heart icons, while, as Barron concludes, "adults wait in the woods to take their profits." [17]

DESIGNED TO DISCRIMINATE

Digital products designed to gather as much information about you as they can, even if that data collection does little to improve your experience. Screens built to be tapped through as quickly as possible, so you won't notice what you're agreeing to. Services that collect information based on proxy, and use it to make (often incorrect) assumptions about you. "Delightful" features designed to hide what's actually under the hood. Patronizing language that treats you like a child—and tries to make you believe that tech companies know best. And that's just scratching the surface. Once you start trying to understand how digital products track your habits and collect your data, it's hard to stop—because there's always some new technology emerging, some new product taking surveillance to an even creepier level.

I'm not a privacy expert either. I can't tell you how to fully detox from data collection; in fact, I think the only way to do it is to stop using digital products altogether. Anything else is just a method for limiting your exposure, for fending off or outsmarting the beast (until some new technology thwarts you again). That doesn't mean it's not worthwhile to keep track of your digital footprint and try to limit your data trail. It just means that we also need to think long and hard about how we got here in the first place.

One reason data collection has become so commonplace, and so intense, is that too many of us have spent the past two decades enamored of the brilliance of technology, and blind to how that technology comes to be. Meanwhile, back at the companies behind those technologies, a world of mostly white men has wholeheartedly embraced the idea that they're truly smarter than the rest of us. That they *do* know best. That they deserve to make choices on our behalf. That there's nothing wrong with watching us in "god view," because they are, in fact, gods. And there's no one around to tell them otherwise, because anyone who's different either shuts up or gets pushed out.

These companies take advantage of our obliviousness at every turn, making design and business decisions that affect us all, without ever actually keeping all of us in mind—without understanding what real people are like, considering our needs, or planning for when things go wrong. Why would they? They're too busy clamoring for endless, unfettered growth to realize they've been standing on others' necks to get it.

This kind of surveillance isn't good for any of us, but it's particularly bad for those who are already marginalized. For example, if you're poor, you're more likely to live in a higher-crime neighborhood, where many residents have bad credit. You're also more likely to rely on a mobile device: according to the Pew Research Center, in 2016, one in five Americans who made less than $30,000 a year accessed the internet only from their phone, versus one in twenty of those with incomes over $75,000.[18] Mobile usage leads to a trove of location-based data being stored about you, and that location data tells businesses where you live and where you spend time. Once that data is digested, you're likely to be showered with "predatory ads for subprime loans or for-profit schools."[19] Plus, it takes a huge amount of time to learn about online tracking and data collection—not to mention the time needed to implement and maintain privacy practices, and the money to invest in additional security programs like password managers.

The only way the technology industry will set reasonable, humane standards for what type of information can be collected and how it can be used is if we stop allowing it to see itself as special—stop allowing it to skirt the law, change the rules, and obfuscate the truth. It's a hard problem, to be sure: much of the modern internet's business model is built on buying, selling, parsing, and mining personal data. But pushback is the only way forward. Because once our data is collected—as messy and incorrect as it often is—it gets fed to a whole host of models and algorithms, each of them spitting out results that serve to make marginalized groups even more vulnerable, and tech titans even more powerful.

Chapter 7
Algorithmic Inequity

On the morning of January 20, 2013, Bernard Parker was pulled over in Broward County, Florida. His tags were expired. During the stop, police found an ounce of marijuana in the twenty-three-year-old's car—enough to charge him with felony drug possession with intent to sell. By 9:30 a.m., he had been booked into jail, where he spent the next twenty-four hours.

One month later, in the predawn hours of February 22, Dylan Fugett was arrested in the same county. He was twenty-four years old. His crime: possession of cocaine, marijuana, and drug paraphernalia. He spent the rest of the night in jail too.

Parker had a prior record. In 2011 he had been charged with resisting arrest without violence—a first-degree misdemeanor in Florida. Police say he ran from them, along the way throwing away a baggie that they suspected contained cocaine. Fugett had a record too: in 2010 he had been charged with felony attempted burglary.[1]

You might think these men have similar criminal profiles:

they're from the same place, born less than a year apart, charged with similar crimes. But according to software called Correctional Offender Management Profiling for Alternative Sanctions, or COMPAS, these men aren't the same at all. COMPAS rated Parker a 10, the highest risk there is for recidivism. It rated Fugett only a 3.

Fugett has since been arrested three more times: twice in 2013, for possessing marijuana and drug paraphernalia, and once in 2015, during a traffic stop, when he was arrested on a bench warrant and admitted he was hiding eight baggies of marijuana in his boxers. Parker hasn't been arrested again at all.

Parker is black. Fugett is white. And according to a 2016 investigation by *ProPublica*, their results are typical: only about six out of ten defendants who COMPAS predicts will commit a future crime actually go on to do so. That figure is roughly the same across races. But the *way* the software is wrong is telling: Black defendants are twice as likely to be falsely flagged as high-risk. And white defendants are nearly as likely to be falsely flagged as low-risk. *ProPublica* concluded that COMPAS, which is used in hundreds of state and local jurisdictions across the United States, is biased against black people.[2]

It's also secret.

COMPAS is made by a private company called Northpointe, and Northpointe sees the algorithms behind the software as proprietary—secret recipes it doesn't want competitors to steal. That's pretty typical. Algorithms now control a huge number of systems that we interact with every day—from which posts bubble to the top of your Facebook feed, to whether image recognition software can correctly identify a person, to what kinds of job ads you see online. And most of those algorithms, like COM-

PAS, are considered proprietary, so we can't see how they've been designed.

COMPAS might be a particularly problematic example—it can directly affect how long a convicted person spends in jail, after all. But it's far from alone. Because, no matter how much tech companies talk about algorithms like they're nothing but advanced math, they always reflect the values of their creators: the programmers and product teams working in tech. And as we've seen time and again, the values that tech culture holds aren't neutral. After all, the same biases that lead teams to launch a product that assumes all its users are straight, or a sign-up form that assumes people aren't multiracial, are what lead them to launch machine-learning products that are just as exclusive and alienating—and, even worse, locked in a black box, where they're all but invisible.

WHAT *IS* AN ALGORITHM?

If you're not exactly sure what "algorithm" means, don't despair. Many of us can use the word in a sentence but can't describe how one works, or precisely why so many of today's digital services rely on algorithms. But don't be fooled: while they can be used to solve complex problems, algorithms themselves can be extremely simple. An algorithm is just the specific set of steps needed to perform some type of computation—*any* type of computation. For example, let's say you want to add two numbers together:

$$57$$
$$+\ 34$$
$$\overline{}$$

You could do what's called the partial-sum method: First you add the numbers in the tens column together, 50 plus 30, for a total of 80. Then you add the numbers in the ones column together, 7 and 4, for a total of 11. Finally, you add those partial sums together, 80 plus 11, for a total of 91. This happens to be more or less how I add sums in my head, though the steps are so ingrained I hardly know I'm doing them. But that's not the only method for solving this problem.

You could also use the column method: first you add the numbers in the ones column, 7 plus 4, for a total of 11. You put the 11 in the ones column of your answer. Then you add the tens column, 5 plus 3, for a total of 8. You put that in the tens column of your answer. But each column can contain only one digit, so you trade ten of your 1's for one 10. This gives you 9 in the tens column, and leaves you with 1 in the ones column. Once again, your total is 91. These are both examples of algorithms: the steps you take to figure something out.

We do algorithms like these all day long. It's just that we don't necessarily think about our day-to-day tasks that way, because we do them automatically. In fact, if you grew up with the kind of public-school education I got in the 1980s and 1990s, you probably didn't learn to add using either of these methods. In my school, we stood up in front of the chalkboard and added up the ones column, and when it was more than 10, we "carried the 1" over to the next column, marking a tiny 1 on top of the tens column as we went. That approach is fundamentally the same as the columns method, except that it speeds through some of the steps, rather than making each one explicit.

Maybe that's why we tend to glaze over when people talk about algorithms. They sound complex, because most of us are not used to breaking down discrete steps in such painstaking detail. But that's what the algorithms behind tech products are doing: they run through a long list of incredibly tedious steps in order to perform a computation. The difference is just that they're doing it at a scale that we humans can't compete with; after all, if you got bored with my breaking down all the tasks required to do column addition, you would never sit down with a pencil and paper and sort out equations with hundreds or thousands of factors. That's what it would take to determine, say, which site comes up first in a Google search, or which of the nearby restaurants bubbles to the top of Yelp's review list when you search on the word "dinner."

That's why computers are so great: data sets that would take individual humans whole lifetimes to make sense of can be sorted through in an instant. But that power isn't without its problems. Because algorithms crunch through so much information at once, it's easy never to think about *how* they do it, or ask whether the answer they spit out at the end is actually accurate. A computer can't get it wrong—right?

Sadly, they can. Computers are extremely good at performing tasks, true. But if a computer is fed a faulty algorithm—given the wrong set of tasks to perform—it won't know that it didn't end up at the right conclusion, unless it gets feedback letting it know it was wrong. Imagine a math teacher accidentally leaving a step out of an addition lesson. The student then has a faulty algorithm—one that results in a wrong answer every time, no matter how perfectly the student performs the steps. That's what happens when an algorithm is biased: the computer isn't failing. The model is.

The algorithm that Yelp uses when you search for "dinner,"

for example, is designed to go through all of the listings in Yelp's database and pick out the ones that are best suited to your search. But Yelp can't actually *know* which restaurant is the best option for you at a given moment, so instead its algorithm uses what it does know, both about you and about the restaurants in its database, to make an educated guess. It does this by taking all the factors that Yelp's product team decided were relevant—restaurants you've reviewed in the past, restaurants you've viewed in the past, how close a restaurant is to you, whether other people tended to say it's good for dinner, whether they used the term "dinner" in their reviews, the total number of reviews the restaurant has, its star rating, and many, many more items—and running them through a proprietary system of weighting and ranking those variables. The result is a prioritized list that helps you, the user, choose a restaurant.

A perfect algorithm would be one in which every single user query produced precisely the ten restaurants that are most likely to make that user happy. That's probably not possible, of course; humans are too diverse, with too many different whims, to satisfy all people, all the time. But it's the ideal. Meanwhile, a faulty algorithm would turn up inappropriate or bad options for users—like consistently recommending businesses that don't serve food, or that other users said were terrible. Mostly, the algorithm is somewhere in the middle: it finds just what you want a lot of the time, but sends you somewhere mediocre some of the time too. Yelp is also able to tune its model and improve results over time, by looking at things like how often users search, don't like the results, and then search again. The algorithm is the core of Yelp's product—it's what connects users to businesses—so you can bet that data scientists are tweaking and refining this model all the time.

A product like COMPAS, the criminal recidivism software, doesn't just affect whether you opt for tacos or try a new ramen place tonight, though. It affects people's lives: whether they can get bail, how long they will spend in prison, whether they'll be eligible for parole. But just like Yelp, COMPAS can't *know* whether an individual is going to commit a future crime. All it has is data that it believes *indicates* they are more or less likely to.

Northpointe calls those indicators "risk and needs factors," and it uses 137 of them in the COMPAS algorithm. Many of those questions focus on the defendant's criminal history: how many times they've been arrested, how many convictions they've had, how long they've spent in jail in the past. But dozens of the questions that COMPAS asks aren't related to crime at all—questions like, "How many times did you move in the last twelve months?" or "How often did you feel bored?" Those 137 answers are fed into the system, and—like magic—a COMPAS risk score ranging from 1 to 10 comes out the other end.

Except, it's not magic. It's a system that's rife with problems. For one, many of these questions focus on whether people in your family or social circle have ever been arrested. According to Northpointe, these factors correlate to a person's risk level. But in the United States, black people are incarcerated at six times the rate of white people—often because of historical biases in policing, from racial profiling to the dramatically more severe penalties for possession of crack compared with possession of cocaine (the same drug) throughout the 1980s and 1990s.[3] So if you're black—no matter how lawfully you act and how careful you are—you're simply a lot more likely to know people who've been arrested. They're your neighbor, your classmate, your dad.

Cathy O'Neil claims that this reliance on historical data is a fundamental problem with many algorithmic systems: "Big data processes codify the past," she writes. "They do not invent the future."[4] So if the past was biased (and it certainly was), then these systems will keep that bias alive—even as the public is led to believe that high-tech models remove human error from the equation. The only way to stop perpetuating the bias is to build a model that takes these historical facts into account, and adjusts to rectify them in the future. COMPAS doesn't.

Then there's the way those 137 questions are asked. According to Northpointe, the software is designed for "test administration flexibility": the agency using the software can choose to ask defendants to fill in their own reports, lead the defendant through an interview and ask the questions verbatim, or hold what it calls a "guided discussion," in which the interviewer uses a "motivational interviewing style" to "enhance rapport and buy-in for the intervention process."[5] That flexibility sounds great for buyers of the software, but it means that agencies are gathering data in varied, nonstandard ways—and that their own biases about offenders, or lack of attention to potential biases, might lead them to assume an answer in the "guided discussion" that a suspect never would have said about themselves.

So that's the data going into the algorithm—the facets that Northpointe says indicate future criminality. But what about the steps that the algorithm itself takes to arrive at a score? It turns out that those have their problems as well. After *Pro-Publica* released its report, several groups of researchers, each working independently at different institutions, decided to take a closer look at *ProPublica*'s findings. They didn't find a clear origin for the bias—a specific piece of the algorithm gone wrong. Instead, they found that *ProPublica* and Northpointe were simply looking at the concept of "fairness" in very different ways.

At Northpointe, fairness was defined as parity in accuracy: the company tuned its model to ensure that people of different races who were assigned the same score also had the same recidivism rates. For example, "among defendants who scored a seven on the COMPAS scale, 60 percent of white defendants reoffended, which is nearly identical to the 61 percent of black defendants who reoffended."[6] At first glance, that makes intuitive sense. But parity in accuracy is only one measure of fairness. As *ProPublica* found, more than twice as many black people as white were labeled high-risk but did not reoffend. What this means is that there may be parity in *accuracy*, but there isn't parity when it comes to the *harm* of incorrect predictions—such as not being allowed bail, or being given a harsher sentence. That harm is shouldered primarily by black defendants.

In fact, researchers at Stanford who looked at *ProPublica*'s data found that, mathematically, when one group has an overall higher arrest rate than another (like black people do, as compared to white people), "it's actually impossible for a risk score to satisfy both fairness criteria at the same time." You can't have parity in accuracy rates *and* parity in the harm of incorrect predictions, because black people are more likely to be arrested, so they are more likely to carry higher scores. As Nathan Srebro, a computer science professor at the University of Chicago and the Toyota Technological Institute at Chicago, puts it, they're "paying the price for the uncertainty" of Northpointe's algorithm.[7]

Despite what Northpointe says, that sure doesn't seem like a fair algorithm to me. So I asked Sorelle Friedler, an assistant professor of computer science at Haverford College and the cochair of a group called Fairness, Accountability, and Transparency in Machine Learning (FAT/ML), how we should look at these sorts of competing "fairness" criteria. According to her, the problem with COMPAS starts not with the algorithm, but with the values that underlie the way that algorithm was designed. "In order to mathematically define fairness, we have to decide what we think fairness should be," she told me. "This is obviously a long-standing, many-thousands-of-years-old question in society: 'What does it mean to be fair?' And, somehow, we have to boil that down to some formula." That's a "necessarily flawed" process, she says. "It will capture some definition of fairness, under some situations, with lots of caveats." [8]

But the underlying problem isn't that algorithms like COMPAS can't perfectly model "fairness." It's that they're not really trying. Instead, they're relying on a definition that sounds nice, without thinking about who is harmed by it and how it might perpetuate the inequities of the past. And they're doing it in private, despite its impact on the public.

That's why COMPAS is such a cautionary tale for the tech industry—and all of us who use tech products. Because, as powerful as algorithms are, they're not inherently "correct." They're just a series of steps and rules, applied to a set of data, designed to reach an outcome. The questions we need to ask are, Who decided what that desired outcome was? Where did the data come from? How did they define "good" or "fair" results? And how might that definition leave people behind? Otherwise, it's far too easy for teams to carry the biases of the past with them into their software, creating algorithms that, at best, make a product less effective for some users—and, at worst, wreak havoc on their lives.

THE NONGORILLA IN THE ROOM

One Sunday in June 2015, Jacky Alciné was sitting in his room watching the BET Awards show, when a photo from a friend popped up in Google Photos. He started playing with the app and saw that all his images had been assigned to new categories: a picture of a jet wing snapped from his seat was tagged with "Airplanes." A photo of his brother in cap and gown was tagged with "Graduation." And a selfie of him and a friend mugging for the camera? It was labeled "Gorillas."

Yep, "Gorillas," a term so loaded with racist history, so prob-

Google Photos' automatic image tagging puts photos into categories for you. It works pretty well—except when it goes horribly wrong. (Jacky Alciné)

lematic, that Alciné felt frustrated the moment he saw it. "Having computers class you as something that black people have been called for centuries" was upsetting, he told Manoush Zomorodi on the WNYC podcast *Note to Self.* "You look like an ape, you've been classified as a creature. . . . That was the underlying thing that triggered me." [9]

And it wasn't just one photo of Alciné and his friend that the app had tagged as gorillas. It was actually every single photo they had taken that day—a whole series of the two of them goofing around at an outdoor concert. "Over fifty of my photos in that set were labeled under the animal tag," Alciné told me, looking back on the incident. "Think about that. It made the mistake and kept making it." [10]

No human had made this decision, of course. The categories were courtesy of Google Photos' autotagging feature, which had recently launched, promising to allow users to "search by what you remember about a photo, no description needed." [11] The

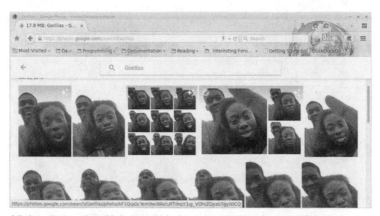

All the photos that Alciné and his friend took that day were labeled as "Gorillas." (Jacky Alciné)

technology is based on deep *neural networks*: massive systems of information that enable machines to "see," much in the same way the human brain does.

Neural networks are built using a *learning algorithm*: rather than being programmed to follow predetermined steps, the algorithm takes historical information, parses it, identifies its patterns, and then uses it to make inferences about new information it encounters. In image processing, it works something like this: millions of images are added to a system, each of them tagged by a human—like "Boston terrier puppy" or "maple tree." Those images make up the system's *training data*: the collection of examples it will learn from. Algorithms then go through the training data and identify patterns.

For example, to build a neural network that could process handwriting, you would need training data with a huge number of different versions of the same letterforms. The idea is that the system would notice that each item tagged as a lowercase "p" had similarities—that they always had a descender immediately connected to a bowl, for example. The wider the range of handwriting used in the training data, the more accurate the system's pattern recognition will be when you let it loose on new data. And once it's accurately identifying new forms of the lowercase "p," those patterns can be added into the network too. This is how a neural network gets smarter over time.[12]

Like our brains, though, computers struggle to understand complex objects, such as photographs, all at once; there are simply too many details and variations to make sense of. Instead they have to learn patterns, like we learned as children. This kind of pattern recognition happens in layers: small details, like the little point at the top of a cat's ear, get connected to larger concepts, like the ear itself, which then gets connected to the larger concept of a cat's head, and so on—until the system builds up enough layers, sometimes twenty or more, to make sense of the full image.[13] The connections between each of those layers are what turn the collection of data into a neural network. Some of these networks are so good that they can even identify an image not just as a car, but also as a particular make, model, and year.[14]

This kind of machine learning is no joke to build. It takes a tremendous amount of training data, plus lots of jiggering, to make the system categorize things correctly. For example, the system might recognize the pointy ears, reddish coloring, and spindly legs of my friend's Portuguese Podengo, compare those details to patterns it has seen before, and mistakenly categorize him as a deer rather than a dog. But the more test data the system has, the less often these kinds of mistakes should happen.

In Alciné's case, the system looked at his selfies and found patterns it recognized too. What made the incident stand out is that those patterns added up to a gorilla. If the error had been different—if the system had thought that Alciné and his friend were bears, for example—he might have chalked it up to a small failure, retagged the images, and moved on. But "gorilla" carries cultural weight—so much, in fact, that Google immediately apologized and told the BBC it was "appalled" that this had happened.[15]

It would be easy to end this anecdote here: all machine-learning systems fail sometimes, and this one just happened to fail in a racially insensitive way. No one *meant* for this to happen. But the bias is actually hidden a lot deeper in the system. Remember, neural networks rely on having a variety of training data to learn how to identify images correctly. That's the only way they get good at their jobs. Now consider what Google's Yonatan Zunger, chief social architect at the time, told Alciné after this incident: "We're also working on longer-term fixes around . . . image recognition itself (e.g., better recognition of dark-skinned faces)," [16] he wrote on Twitter.

Wait a second. Why wasn't Google's image recognition feature as good at identifying dark-skinned faces as it was at identifying light-skinned faces when it launched? And why didn't anyone notice the problem *before* it launched? Well, because failing to design for black people isn't new. It's been happening in photo technology for decades.

Starting back in the 1950s, Kodak, which made most of the film used in the United States, was forced to break up its monopoly on photo processing—so rather than taking your film to Kodak to be developed, you could take it to an independent photo lab. So, Kodak developed a printer that would work for these small labs, and started sending out kits to aid photo technicians in developing their film properly. One item in the kit was the "Shirley Card"—a card depicting a woman in a high-contrast outfit, labeled with the word "normal," surrounded by versions of the same photo with various color problems. Named for the first person to sit for these cards, Shirley Page, a Kodak employee at the time, the cards were used to calibrate skin tones, shadows, and light.[17] Decade after decade, new women would sit for these cards. They were always referred to as "Shirley." And they were always white.

Not only were photo lab technicians calibrating their work to match Shirley's version of normal, but the film itself wasn't designed to work for black customers. Film emulsions—the coat-

One of Kodak's "Shirley Cards,"
showing "normal"—and always
white—skin tones. (Courtesy of
Kodak and Hermann Zschiegner)

ings on one side of film that contain tiny, light-sensitive crys-
tals—"*could* have been designed initially with more sensitivity to
the continuum of yellow, brown, and reddish skin tones," writes
Lorna Roth, a professor of communications at Concordia
University—but only if Kodak had been motivated to recognize
"a more dynamic range" of people. Black customers weren't recognized as an important enough demographic for Kodak to market to, so no one bothered.[18]

Roth notes that this only started to change in the 1970s—but
not necessarily because Kodak was trying to improve its product
for diverse audiences. Earl Kage, who managed Kodak Research
Studios at the time, told her, "It was never Black flesh that was
addressed as a serious problem that I knew of at the time."[19]

Instead, Kodak decided it needed its film to better handle color variations because furniture retailers and chocolate makers had started complaining: they said differences between wood grains, and between milk-chocolate and dark-chocolate varieties, weren't rendering correctly. Improving the product for black audiences was just a by-product.

In the dustup over the "gorillas" incident, Zunger, the Google engineer, even told Alciné on Twitter that "different contrast processing [is] needed for different skin tones and lighting." [20] That's true, but it's not news: it's the same problem that existed for Kodak six decades ago, and that black people have known about for years.

It's not just Google Photos that has failed to make facial-recognition products work as well for people of color as they do for white people. In 2015, Flickr's automatic image tagging labeled a black man as "ape" (not to mention, the gates of Dachau as a "jungle gym").[21] Back in 2009, Nikon released a camera with a special feature: it would warn you if someone in a photo had blinked. The problem was that it hadn't been tested well enough on Asian eyes, and as a result, it routinely flagged them as blinking.[22] That same year, there was the HP computer with a camera that used facial-recognition software to move with the user—panning and zooming to keep their face front and center. Unless the user was black—in which case the software often couldn't recognize them at all.[23]

And yet, several years later—and after huge leaps forward in machine-learning capabilities—Google Photos was making the same mistakes. Why? The answer is right back in those tech-company offices we encountered in Chapter 2. If you recall, Google reported that just 1 percent of technical staff was black in

2016. If the team that made this product looked like Google as a whole, it would have been made up almost entirely of white and Asian men. Would they have noticed if, like COMPAS, their failure rates disproportionately affected black people?

Just adding more people of color to the team won't fix the problem, though. Sorelle Friedler, the computer science professor who studies fairness, says the problem is actually more insidious than that.

> Part of what machine learning is designed to do is find patterns in data. So, often, what you're really seeing are societal patterns being reflected back. In order to remove that, or even notice that it's a problem, it requires a certain perspective that I do think women and minorities are more likely to bring to the table. But in order to do something about it, it requires new algorithmic techniques.[24]

In other words, regardless of the makeup of the team behind an algorithmically powered product, people must be trained to think more carefully about the data they're working with, and the historical context of that data. Only then will they ask the right questions—like, "Is our training data representative of a range of skin tones?" and "Does our product fail more often for certain kinds of images?"—and, critically, figure out how to adjust the system as a result.

Without those questions, it's no surprise that the Google Photos algorithm didn't learn to identify dark-skinned faces very well: because at Google, just like at Kodak in the 1950s, "normal" still defaults to white.

BIASED INPUT, EVEN MORE BIASED OUTPUT

When Alciné started tweeting about his experience with Google Photos, some people were as angry as he was. Others replied with racist comments; it's the internet, after all. But a lot of people rolled their eyes and said that he shouldn't be offended—that "computers can't be racist," and "you can't blame Google for it; machines are stupid."

That sentiment is echoed from within the tech companies that specialize in image recognition too: in 2016, Moshe Greenshpan, the CEO of the facial-recognition software company Face-Six, told *Motherboard* writer Rose Eveleth that he can't worry about "little issues" like Alciné's. "I don't think my engineers or other companies' engineers have any hidden agenda to give more attention to one ethnicity," he told her. "It's just a matter of practical use cases." [25]

Sound familiar? That's the classic edge-case thinking we looked at back in Chapter 3—thinking that allows companies to shrug their shoulders at all the people whose identities aren't whatever their narrow definition of "normal" is. But Alciné and his friend aren't edge cases. They're people—customers who deserve to have a product that works just as well for them as for anyone else.

There's also a special danger in writing off "edge cases" in algorithmic systems as impractical and not worth designing for—because that write-off may not end there. It's not just that Alciné and his friend get coded as gorillas. It's that a system, left uncorrected, will keep making those mistakes, over and over, and think it's getting things right. Without feedback—without people like Alciné taking it upon themselves to retag their photos manually—the system won't get better over time.

It can actually get worse.

In 2013, Google researchers trained a system to comb through Google News articles, parsing huge amounts of text and identifying patterns in how words are used within them. The result is Word2vec, a neural network made up of 3 million *word embeddings*, or semantic relationships between words. What Word2vec does is essentially reconstruct the way words work linguistically, in order to improve capabilities for *natural language processing*: the practice of teaching machines to understand human language as it's spoken or written day to day—the kind of thing that allows Siri or a search engine to understand what you mean and provide an answer. Word2vec and other similar word-embedding systems do this by looking at how frequently pairs of words appear in the same text, and how near each other they appear. Over time, these patterns allow a system to understand semantic meaning and accurately complete analogies like "man is to woman as king is to _____" or "Paris is to France as Tokyo is to _____." [26]

That's all well and good, but the system also returns other kinds of relationships—like "man is to woman as computer programmer is to homemaker." This is because word embeddings show a strong vector between "man" and "computer programmer," which is similar to the vector between "woman" and "homemaker." The same is true for "father is to doctor as mother is to nurse," "man is to architect as woman is to interior designer," and even "man is to coward as woman is to whore." When you think about it, these pairings aren't very surprising: There *are* more women who are nurses than doctors. Computer programmers *do* still tend to be male. So it makes sense that these cultural realities are also depicted in news articles; for example, journalists routinely use job titles to describe a person being quoted.

In other words, if a system like Word2vec is fed data that reflects historical biases, then those biases will be reflected in the resulting word embeddings. The problem is that very few people have been talking about this—and meanwhile, because Google released Word2vec as an open-source technology, all kinds of companies are using it as the foundation for other products. These products include recommendation engines (the tools behind all those "you might also like . . ." features on websites), document classification, and search engines—all without considering the implications of relying on data that reflects historical biases and outdated norms to make future predictions.

One of the most worrisome developments is this: using word embeddings to automatically review résumés. That's what a company called Talla, which makes artificial-intelligence software, reported it was doing in 2016. Called CV2vec, this software can "find candidates that are most similar to a reference person or the job ad itself, cluster people together and visualize how CVs align with each other, and even make a prediction as to what someone's next job will be" [27]—all without a human ever looking at their résumé. According to Talla CEO Rob May, the results could make it easier for companies to identify candidates that most match up with current top-performing staff: "What if you could say 'I want someone like my best engineer, but with more experience in management?'" [28]

Well, if that query were based on word embeddings derived from historical texts—such as the résumés of engineers already on staff—you just might end up discarding applications from women engineers, because your training data connected the term "engineer" more closely to male attributes than to female ones. For example, the system might notice that the current engineers' names reflected certain patterns, or that those engineers tended to be part of a specific fraternity, and therefore decide that candidates who also have traditionally male names or were in a fraternity are a better match for the position. And because word embeddings are part of a complex network, the words "man" and "woman" don't need to be present anywhere for this to happen.

That's what concerns researchers from Boston University and Microsoft Research about artificial intelligence based on word embeddings. In a paper titled "Man Is to Computer Programmer as Woman Is to Homemaker? Debiasing Word Embeddings," they argue that because word embeddings frequently underpin a range of other machine-learning systems, they "not only reflect such stereotypes but can also amplify them"[29]—effectively bringing the bias of the original data set to new products and new data sets. So much for machines being neutral.

This doesn't mean we need to throw out technology like Word2vec. It just means that tech companies have to work harder. Either they need to get a lot better at feeding these systems unbiased text or, more feasibly, they need to make it part of their job to scrub the bias from word embeddings before using them. The latter is what the researchers from Boston University and Microsoft propose. They demonstrate a method for algorithmically debiasing word embeddings, ensuring that gender-neutral words, like "nurse," are not embedded closer to women than to men—without breaking the appropriate gender connection between words like "man" and "father." They also argue that the same could be done with other types of stereotypes, such as racial bias.

Once again, the problem isn't with the technology. It's with the assumptions that technologists so often make: that the data they have is neutral, and that anything at the edges can be written off. And once those assumptions are made, they wrap them up in a pretty, polished software package, making it even harder for everyone else to understand what's actually happening under the surface.

PAY NO ATTENTION TO THE MATH BEHIND THE CURTAIN

In 2012, a seventeen-year-old in South Carolina named Dylann Roof kept hearing about a black teenager who had been shot to death by a security guard in Florida. He googled the name: Trayvon Martin. Roof then read Martin's Wikipedia page, where a phrase caught his eye: "black on white crime." He googled that phrase, and soon he had found his way to the website of the Council of Conservative Citizens, the largest white-supremacist group in the United States.[30]

"I have never been the same since that day," Roof wrote in an online manifesto in 2015. "There were pages upon pages of these brutal black on White murders. I was in disbelief."[31] He dug further, his searches leading him deeper and deeper into the world of online hate groups and propaganda. He discovered the "Jewish problem." And then he decided to do something with his newfound "racial awareness." At 4:44 on the afternoon of June 17, 2015, he finished the manifesto.

That evening, he entered Charleston's historic Emanuel

African Methodist Episcopal Church, and sat with members of a Bible study group for an hour. Then he stood up, opened fire, and killed nine black people.

Roof's case is extreme, tragic, and terrifying. But it highlights just how much influence technology—and the way technology is designed—has over what people believe is true. That's not by accident, writes sociologist Miriam E. Sweeney. She claims it's an explicit part of Google's design, which "frames the search process as informational, unbiased, and scientific." [32] She writes:

> The simple, sparse design works to obscure the complexity of the interface, making the result appear purely scientific and data-driven. This is an image Google actively cultivates. The company has explicitly claimed its results to be neutral, standing behind the authority of its "objective" algorithmic ranking system. . . . The insistence of the scientific "truth" of algorithmic search has encouraged users to view search as an objective and neutral experience.

By and large, people *do* trust Google: back in 2012, when Roof began his search for race-related information, the Pew Research Center reported that nearly three in four search engine users in the United States said that "most or all the information they find as they use search engines is accurate and trustworthy," and two out of three believed "search engines are a fair and unbiased source of information." [33] According to a 2017 report by the communications marketing firm Edelman, that's still largely the case: in a survey of 33,000 people conducted worldwide during the fall of 2016, 64 percent said they trusted search engines for news and information—seven points more than the 57 percent of respondents who said they trusted traditional media.[34]

This isn't by accident. In his book *In The Plex: How Google Thinks, Works, and Shapes Our Lives*, author Stephen Levy describes how Marissa Mayer once rejected a design at Google: "It looks like a human was involved in choosing what went where. It looks too editorialized," she told the team of designers. "Google products are machine-driven. They're created by machines. And that is what makes us powerful. That's what makes our products great."[35]

It's not just search that relies on a clean, simple aesthetic. We can see this same design technique across the platforms and products that rely on algorithms—even in an institutional, niche piece of software like COMPAS. Northpointe bills COMPAS as "simple to use and interpret," saying that it's "designed to be user-friendly, even for those with limited computer experience and education."[36] And it shows in the interface itself, which transforms a person's specific story into a series of color-coded bar charts.

In consumer software, the design aesthetic is even stronger: just try not to be mesmerized while watching your sleek little car arrive on Uber, or seeing your photos instantly sort into tidy little categories in Google Photos. Again, Uber stops being a company with thousands upon thousands of contingent workers who sleep in their cars and work sixteen-hour days to make ends meet, and starts being nothing but a slick app that magically transports you from A to B. Google Photos stops being a complex, algorithmically driven system, and starts feeling like an objective truth.

Now, I spend most days running a consulting firm that helps

companies simplify their content, strip interfaces of extra steps, and generally produce technology that makes more sense for the people who have to use it. I believe that making interfaces easier to use is vital work. But when designers use clean aesthetics to cover over a complex reality—to take something human, nuanced, and rife with potential for bias, and flatten it behind a seamless interface—they're not really making it *easier* for you. They're just hiding the flaws in their model, and hoping you won't ask too many difficult questions.

ARTIFICIAL INTELLIGENCE, REAL IMPACT

This stuff might sound advanced, but odds are good that it's already affecting your everyday life. Whenever you go online, you're almost certain to encounter algorithmically generated results. They decide what you'll be prompted to read next when you reach the bottom of an article. They tell you which products "people like you" tend to purchase. They control your Google results and your Netflix recommendations. They're why you see only a portion of your friends' posts on your Facebook News Feed.

Algorithmic models are also used behind the scenes in all kinds of industries: to evaluate teachers' performance, to find fraudulent activity on an account, to determine how much your insurance should cost, to decide whether you should be approved for a loan. The list could go on and on.

In all of these places, algorithms are making choices that affect your life, from whether you can find or keep a job to how much you pay for a product to what information you can access. And every single one of them is subject to the kinds of biases mentioned here. Add in the fact that all of these algorithms rely on personal data—*your* data—and the disconnect between just how much power these systems have, compared with how little the general public knows about them, is downright scary.

Even more worrisome, most of the people who create these products aren't considering the harm that their work could do to people who aren't like them. It's not because they're consciously biased, though, according to University of Utah computer science professor Suresh Venkatasubramanian. They're just not thinking about it—because it has never occurred to them that it's something *to* think about. "No one really spends a lot of time thinking about privilege and status," he told *Motherboard*. "If you are the defaults you just assume you just are." [37]

According to Sorelle Friedler, one of the biggest concerns is the training data—the data used to build these models in the first place. Training data includes things like the images that Google Photos was fed before it launched, or the text corpus that Word2vec consumed to build its embeddings, or the historical crime data that COMPAS crunched to determine its model. "There's not enough focus on what specific data is being used to create the tools," Friedler told me. "If someone is creating a recidivism prediction algorithm that uses rearrest data as the outcome variable, then what they are actually doing is creating a prediction tool to determine who will be rearrested—which potentially bears little relationship to who actually recommitted a crime." [38]

To demonstrate, she related a story she had heard from a defense lawyer, who worries about algorithms because they're often trained using data about parole violations as a primary factor; that is, if you violate parole, you're much more likely to get a high-risk score. The lawyer had a client who was told he couldn't own guns while on parole. The man went home, got his guns, and took them to a pawnshop. Police were staking out the shop. They arrested him and called the incident a violation—even though he was complying with the conditions of his parole. "As soon as you start training the algorithm to that type of thing, then you have to ask, 'Who is more likely to be caught?'" said Friedler. "People need to understand that data is not truth. It is not going to magically solve these hard societal problems for us." [39]

At the same time, Friedler cautions that the answer isn't to throw up our hands and say, "We tried those data-driven things, and it turns out that they're bad, so we'll go back to not thinking about data." Data matters.

Or at least, *good* data does. If we want to build a society that's fairer, more just, and more inclusive than in the past, then blindly accepting past data as neutral—as an accurate, or desirable, model upon which to build the future—won't cut it. We need to demand instead that the tech industry take responsibility for the data it collects. We need it to be transparent about where that data comes from, which assumptions might be encoded in it, and whether it represents users equally. Otherwise, we'll only encounter more examples of products built on biased machine learning in the future. And as we're about to see, when problematic algorithms mix with weaknesses built into digital platforms themselves, their ramifications can be profound.

Chapter 8
Built to Break

Lindy West is used to online hate. A comedian and author best known for writing about feminism and being fat, she's a pro at ignoring taunts about her weight, her career, and her politics. But when a picture of a Thomas the Tank Engine character with the words "CHOO CHOO MOTHERFUCKER THE RAPE TRAIN'S ON ITS WAY. NEXT STOP YOU" pasted on top showed up in her Twitter mentions in 2014, she felt creeped out and menaced. So, West took the only action available to her: she reported it as abuse.

At the time, Twitter's terms of service specifically stated that "users may not make direct, specific threats of violence against others"—yet West was told her experience didn't qualify. "We've investigated the account and the Tweets reported as abusive behavior, and have found that it's currently not violating the Twitter Rules," said the response from Twitter's support team.[1]

It wasn't just West. As soon as she posted a screenshot of the tweet and Twitter's response, she heard from countless other women who'd had their reports of abusive tweets rejected as well. The tweets deemed OK by Twitter? They included everything from rape and death threats to suggestions of suicide to a troll telling a woman, "I would love to knock you the fuck out."

By early 2015, West's article had made the rounds at Twitter, and even then-CEO Dick Costolo took notice. "We suck at dealing with abuse and trolls on the platform and we've sucked at it for years," he wrote in a memo to staff. "We lose core user after core user by not addressing simple trolling issues that they face every day." [2]

Costolo was right: in a 2014 Pew Research Center study, 13 percent of people who'd been harassed online said they had deleted a profile or changed their username because of harassment, and 10 percent said they had left an online forum because of it. [3]

After two more years of sustained harassment, that's precisely what West did. In January 2017—as then-president-elect Donald Trump was taunting South Korea and strangers were harassing her for her views on the death of Carrie Fisher—West realized she was *done*: She was tired of neo-Nazis digging into her personal life. She was tired of men telling her they'd like to rape her, "if [she] weren't so fat." More than anything, she was tired of feeling like all Twitter's talk about taking harassment seriously hadn't gotten her anywhere:

> I talk back and I am "feeding the trolls." I say nothing and the harassment escalates. I report threats and I am a "censor." I use mass-blocking tools to curb abuse and I am abused further for blocking "unfairly." [4]

Twitter had helped West build a national audience for her writing. It had helped her turn her memoir, *Shrill*, into a best-selling book. In many ways, it had been the most visible part of her professional profile: she had almost 100,000 followers. But it just wasn't worth it anymore. She deactivated her account.

The first piece of advice anyone gets about online harassment is the same line that West finally got sick of: Don't feed the trolls. Don't read the comments. Online spaces are simply filled with shitheads and pot stirrers, the story goes, so there's no point in trying to do anything about it. Just ignore them and they'll move on. This is untrue: harassment campaigns can last months, even when victims *do* ignore the perpetrators. But this advice is also a subtle form of misdirection: by focusing attention on what the victim does or doesn't do, it diverts attention away from why the abuse happens in the first place—and how digital platforms themselves enable that abuse.

It's not just harassment either. The digital platforms we rely on to connect with friends, stay informed, and build our careers are routinely being manipulated in ways that harm us—from the abuse that women like West routinely receive, to Facebook's Trending algorithm being inundated with fake news during the 2016 election, to the way Reddit's system of subreddits puts the burden of oversight on unpaid moderators and makes it impossible to keep harassing and creepy content out.

It's no accident that so many digital platforms can be so easily exploited by the worst among us. In fact, it's by their very design.

It's not that their founders intended to build platforms that cause harm. But every digital product bears the fingerprints of its creators. Their values are embedded in the ways the systems operate: in the basic functions of the software, in the features they prioritize (and the ones they don't), and in the kind of relationship they expect from you. And as we've seen throughout this book, when those values reflect a narrow worldview—one defined by privileged white men dead set on "disruption" at all costs—things fall apart for everyone else.

In this chapter we'll look at the origins of three platforms that were built with, mostly, good intentions—but that have broken in dangerous ways: Twitter, Reddit, and Facebook. How have the values and biases of each of their creators fundamentally shaped the way these platforms work—and the ways they don't?

THE DOWNSIDE TO AN UPDATE

On July 18, 2016, Milo Yiannopoulos—then an editor at the ultraconservative *Breitbart News*, and the self-proclaimed "most fabulous supervillain on the internet"—published his review of the new, women-led *Ghostbusters* movie. No one expected it to be kind; this is someone who had regularly published articles like "Birth Control Makes Women Unattractive and Crazy" and "Fat People Should Absolutely Hate Themselves," after all. Plus, he'd been posting sneering speculation about the film since he'd called the preview "screechingly terrible" back in May.

The review lived up—or, more accurately, down—to expectations: he called the stars "teenage boys with tits," the script an "abomination," and the audience "lonely middle-aged women." He insisted that feminists "can only survive by sucking on the teat of Big Government." He suggested the women should have fought "a giant tub of Ben & Jerry's" while crying and watching romantic comedies. He cracked jokes deriding lesbians.[5]

In other words, like everything Yiannopoulos writes, the review was designed to whip his cultlike following of young men into a froth.

It worked: within hours, his fans took to Twitter to harass comedian Leslie Jones, who played Patty in the film. They called her ugly, manly, and unfunny. They called her an "ape," a "big lipped coon," and scads of other racist names. They even sent photos doctored to look like she had semen on her face. Jones shared the offensive messages she was getting with her followers. She reported the abuse to Twitter. She blocked users who attacked her. But it just wouldn't stop.

Meanwhile, Yiannopoulos started tweeting out fake screenshots of offensive tweets that he claimed were from Jones's account. Once his 388,000 followers got hold of them, the abusive tweets only got worse. By the end of the day, Jones was a wreck. "I feel like I'm in a personal hell," she tweeted just after midnight. "I didn't do anything to deserve this. It's just too much." Within the hour, she had announced she'd be leaving Twitter for a while, "with tears and a very sad heart."[6]

This wasn't the first time Yiannopoulos had led a campaign to harass a woman on Twitter; he'd been directing his followers to attack his "opponents" since the "Gamergate" campaign of 2014, in which women video game developers were systematically targeted with rape and death threats. But it turned out to be the last: on July 20, 2016, Twitter permanently banned him from the service.

What happened to Jones was horrific. But as Lindy West's story more than a year and a half earlier shows us, it was far from new. Twitter has been home to abusive behavior since its founding in 2007—much of it misogynist, racist, or both.

What was new was Twitter's response. In a statement after banning Yiannopoulos, the microblogging service announced it would be stepping up measures to prevent harassment on the site:

> Many people believe we have not done enough to curb this type of behavior on Twitter. We agree. We are continuing to invest heavily in improving our tools and enforcement systems to better allow us to identify and take faster action on abuse as it's happening and prevent repeat offenders.[7]

Twitter released the first major results of this effort in November 2016, when it launched features that allow users to mute specific keywords from appearing in their feeds, or to mute entire conversations they've been tagged in—helpful if, for example, a harasser includes your username in a Tweet to their followers, and those followers reply with a whole series of harassing messages of their own. At the same time, Twitter also made it easier for users to report accounts for being abusive or harmful, and said it was working on internal processes for evaluating and responding to those reports.[8]

In early 2017, Ed Ho, the vice president of engineering, promised that "making Twitter a safer place is our primary focus and we are now moving with more urgency than ever." A few days later, another round of improvements rolled out: tools to better prevent people who have been banned from creating a new profile; a "safe search" that removes potentially sensitive content and tweets from people you've blocked or muted; and a content filter that collapses replies to a tweet that it thinks are abusive or low-quality.[9] As I write this, Twitter is promising that even more features are on the way.

But Yiannopoulos spent the rest of 2016 busy too. The day he was banned from Twitter, he showed up at the Republican National Convention in Cleveland wearing a bulletproof vest and the biggest grin you've ever seen. Because by this point, being banned wasn't a problem. It was a blessing. "It's fantastic," he told writer Laurie Penny that day. "It's the end of the platform. The timing is perfect. I thought I had another six months, but this was always going to happen."[10]

The reason Yiannopoulos was so gleeful was simple: he'd already gotten what he needed from Twitter. He had an audience of angry young men ready to do his bidding. And being banned gave him a new way to cry victim—to cast himself as a free-speech crusader silenced by the lefties in Silicon Valley. On that day, his status as a poster child for the alt-right movement—or, as those of us unwilling to sugarcoat call it, neofascism—seemed cemented. He had won.

After the convention, Yiannopoulos took his signature brand of bronze-skinned, designer-sunglassed nihilism on a college speaking tour. In December 2016, at the University of Wisconsin–Milwaukee, he put the name and photo of a trans-gender student up on the screen behind him, and proceeded to mock her, misgender her, and tell the crowd that she was actually just trying to force herself into women's locker rooms. The woman, Adelaide Kramer, was in the audience that night. She was petrified. "I didn't know if I was going to get attacked or not. I was just like, 'Dear god, I hope nobody recognizes me,'" she told *Broadly*.[11]

In February 2017, Yiannopoulos was also invited to speak at

UC Berkeley—where, according to a number of media outlets, he planned to use his time on stage to reveal the names and personal information of students who are undocumented immigrants.[12] He never got a chance: 1,500 people came to protest, and a small group of "black bloc" protesters—masked, anarchist demonstrators—turned it into a riot, breaking windows and setting fires. His speech was canceled. His fans were outraged—including Donald Trump himself, who tweeted, "If U.C. Berkeley does not allow free speech and practices violence on innocent people with a different point of view—NO FEDERAL FUNDS?"[13] Yiannopoulos might have been banned from Twitter, but his power to harm others? It was going strong. (At least until later that month, when a 2016 video of Yiannopoulos condoning pedophilia resurfaced, and he lost both a lucrative book deal and his *Breitbart* job.)

Racist, antiwoman agitators like Yiannopoulos are often framed as having sprung up in 2016—part of a presidential election that broke every rule in the book. But if we want to understand this story, we have to go back much further, long before even Gamergate or Lindy West's harassment. We have to start with the idea of Twitter itself.

Most social networks are built on the concept of reciprocal relationships: a user requests to be your friend on Facebook, or your connection on LinkedIn, and you either approve or deny that request. Twitter, in contrast, is nonreciprocal by default: unless you specifically lock down your account as private, anyone can follow you, or tweet at you—no prior approval needed.

That's because Twitter's central organizing principle isn't *relationships*. It's *updates*. "It started with a fascination with cities and how they work, and what's going on in them right now," recalled cofounder Jack Dorsey in an *LA Times* interview in 2009. He started by tinkering with visualizations of all the people who were roaming a city at a given moment, squawking their whereabouts and activities into CB radios or over cell phones: bicycle messengers, truck couriers, taxis, and emergency vehicles. "But it's missing the public. It's missing normal people," he realized.[14] That's the gap Twitter aimed to fill: "real-time, up-to-date, from the road" posts, "akin to updating your [instant messenger] status from wherever you are, and sharing it," Dorsey wrote back in the spring of 2006, when he shared an early sketch of the service, then in a private beta release, on Flickr.[15]

People loved it. At the 2007 South by Southwest Interactive conference the following spring, thousands of tech startups and bloggers started using the service—and suddenly, the platform jumped from sending 20,000 to 60,000 messages per day.[16] It wasn't long before Twitter became a household name for all kinds of people—most of them looking very little like the four young, white men from San Francisco who'd founded the company. By 2009, women were using the service about as frequently as men. By 2010, the platform had seen massive growth: 50 million tweets were being sent per day by March, compared to just 2.5 million a day in January 2009. That influx of new users was more diverse too: in 2010, just 5 percent of white internet users in the United States were on Twitter, while 13 percent of black internet users were. By 2011, that gap was even larger: a full 25 percent of black American internet users reported being on Twitter, compared with just 9 percent of white American internet users.[17]

In the early days, Twitter's "status updates" concept was explicitly stated in the interface itself, which described the service as "a global community of friends and strangers answering one simple question: What are you doing?"[18] Only, the more Twitter grew, the less often people's tweets answered that question. Because, it turns out, all those "normal people" that Dorsey hoped to attract to Twitter didn't just want to broadcast where they were getting lunch or when they were leaving for work in the morning. They also wanted to banter, share news, tell jokes, make friends, promote their work, and a million other things. As they did, they developed their own techniques for communicating, like adding "RT" to the beginning of a tweet to signify that it was a retweet of someone else's post.

Twitter responded by building many of those features into the product: retweets became a button rather than a manual copy-paste. Link shortening became standard, so that long URLs wouldn't take up half of a tweet's 140-character limit. Users started tagging conversations about a specific topic with a hashtag, like #design, so Twitter added a feature that automatically linked hashtags to a search page listing every tweet that included that tag.

But during all of these product improvements, Twitter built precious few features to prevent or stop the abuse that had become commonplace on the platform. For example, the ability to report a tweet as abusive didn't come until a full six years after the company's founding, in 2013—and then only after Caroline Criado-Perez, a British woman who had successfully led a campaign to get Jane Austen onto the £10 note, was the target of an abuse campaign that generated fifty rape threats *per hour*.[19] By then, it wasn't just Criado-Perez who was experiencing high-volume, high-profile harassment on the platform. Abuse was everywhere—and Twitter, long touting itself "the free speech wing of the free speech party,"[20] had little interest in moderating it.

By the summer of 2014, abuse on Twitter had crescendoed into Gamergate, an episode that, on its face, was about "ethics in video game journalism"—but, at its core, was a sustained, months-long harassment campaign. It started when an ex-boyfriend of game developer Zoe Quinn released a series of manifesto-like blog posts about the ways Quinn had wronged him, insisting that Quinn had cheated on him with industry journalists to get favorable reviews of her game, *Depression Quest*. What it became was a mob of thousands spewing rape and death threats at a series of women involved in video games—threats that were so specific, and so violent, that Quinn and others, like feminist video game critic Anita Sarkeesian, felt unsafe in their homes.[21] And who was stoking this movement? None other than Milo Yiannopoulos, who wrote a series of pro-Gamergate articles on *Breitbart*, using Twitter to specifically call out and threaten women involved.

"Twitter has not just tolerated abuse and hate speech, it's virtually been optimized to accommodate it," concluded *BuzzFeed News* writer Charlie Warzel in August 2016. Warzel had just spent months talking with past employees at Twitter—employees who called the platform "a honeypot for assholes" and said that the product, with its nonreciprocal relationships and anything-goes approach to speech, was "basically built for maximum ease of trolling."[22]

The root of the problem, one former senior employee told Warzel, was precisely what we've seen elsewhere in this book: a homogenous leadership team that spent years "tone-deaf to the concern of users in the outside world, meaning women and people of color." Another, a former engineering manager named Leslie Miley, added, "If Twitter had people in the room who'd been abused on the internet—meaning not just straight, white males—when they were creating the company, I can assure you the service would be different."[23]

It's not that Twitter's founders had bad intentions. It's that they built a product centered on a specific vision: an open platform for short updates from anyone, about anything. And because abuse wasn't really on their radar, they didn't spend much time working out how to prevent it—or even take it seriously when it happened. It wasn't part of the vision.

It wasn't part of the vision, that is, until Twitter started to fail.

Reports on the death of Twitter have been commonplace since late 2015,[24] when, two years after the company went public, efforts to increase user numbers had stalled, and the company posted a net quarterly loss of $132 million.[25] According to many in the industry, Twitter's failure to fix its abuse problem is part of the reason why it's struggling—and why no one wants to buy the company, despite Twitter's best efforts to sell. In 2016, Alphabet (Google's parent company) turned them down. Then, so did both Salesforce and Disney—both, at least in part, because of Twitter's reputation for harassment. According to sources who spoke with *Bloomberg*, Disney pulled out of talks "out of concern that bullying and other uncivil forms of communication on the social media site might soil the company's wholesome family image."[26] Around the same time, CNBC's *Mad Money* host Jim Cramer said that Salesforce CEO Marc Benioff was turned off of the company by "the hatred," and said Salesforce was concerned that "the haters reduce the value of the company."[27]

As of this writing, Twitter is still releasing update after update finally aimed at curbing abuse on the platform. The problem now is that many of those updates are ill considered and hastily made. One example is Twitter lists: lists allow any user to create a collection of accounts that it wants to track together. For example, let's say you run a magazine. You might create a list of all the Twitter users who are magazine staff and freelancers so you can more easily retweet them or track conversations about the magazine. Other users can also subscribe to lists. For example, if you're a fan of a magazine, you might subscribe to a list of its contributors so you can easily keep up with their posts.

But being put on a list isn't always benign. In the real world, lists are often used as a tool for abuse; for example, a troll might add a bunch of women to a list called "feminazi watch list," and then share it with all their friends. Suddenly, a group of trolls is monitoring the women on that list—creating the perfect breeding ground for harassment.

In the past, you'd be notified if someone added you to a list. But in February 2017, Twitter changed things: "We want you to get notifications that matter," the company announced. "Starting today, you won't get notified when you are added to a list." [28] The idea was simple: getting notifications that you'd been added to an abusive list could be frustrating, so Twitter decided the best course of action was to remove all list addition notifications.

The backlash was immediate: "This is sweeping a problem under the rug," replied one user. "This is blinding the vulnerable," said another. "When I get added to lists with names like 'stupid bitches' I would like to be notified. Or not added at all," yet another added.

Two hours later, Twitter killed the change. "This was a misstep. We're rolling back the change and we'll keep listening," the company tweeted.[29]

I'm glad Twitter canceled this change. But the fact is that teams invested time and money in making a system modification and announcing it to the world. They updated code. They updated email systems. They updated help documentation. All without seeing the massive flaws in their plan. Because, for all of Twitter's sudden interest in safety—and despite plenty of people who undoubtedly have good intentions working on the product— the company is still, at its core, driven by a vision that makes sense for the people who designed it, and fails far too easily for many of the rest of us.

AWFULNESS, IN MODERATION

Twitter is the place where some of the worst online harassment plays out, but it's often not where that harassment brews. For that, we turn to Reddit, the popular social news site where users create forums around a topic. These topical forums are called subreddits, and there are thousands of them—from general categories like "r/politics" to niches like "r/britishproblems." In each of these subreddits, anyone can submit and vote on content anonymously.

If you're not a Reddit user—or "Redditor," in the parlance of the site—then you might think it's some kind of fringe community. But it's actually known as "the front page of the internet"— the place where millions of people start their day online. In 2016, it was the seventh most popular site in the United States, garnering north of half a billion visits from more than 250 million unique people each month. For reference, that puts its popularity, as of this writing, somewhere just behind Wikipedia—in other words, not very niche at all.[30]

It's also, in the words of journalist Sarah Jeong, "a flaming garbage pit."[31]

Like Twitter, Reddit was founded with a vision of free speech: anonymous users posting and sharing content about whatever topics they chose. When it launched in 2005, all posts appeared on a general Reddit homepage. Other users could then vote each post up or down, so that—in theory, at least—the best content made it to the top of the page. But as traffic grew, Reddit's founders, Alexis Ohanian and Steve Huffman—then in their early twenties, just a few months out of college at the University of Virginia—started fielding complaints: people interested in programming reported that the content they wanted was no longer surfacing to the top, so they couldn't find it. Ohanian and Huffman responded by creating "r/programming," the very first subreddit.

But, like much of the internet, it didn't take long for subreddits to turn offensive. For years, Reddit hosted forums like "r/jailbait," which featured sexualized photos of teen girls stolen from their social media profiles; "r/creepshots," where users posted "upskirts" and other sexualized photos of women that had been taken secretly; "r/beatingwomen," which featured graphic depictions of violence against women; and "r/coontown," an openly racist, antiblack community.

A few patently awful subreddits were shut down over the years—such as r/jailbait, in 2011, and r/creepshots, in 2012. But it wasn't until June 2015, ten years after it launched, that Reddit started enforcing a more thorough antiharassment policy: "We will ban subreddits that allow their communities to use the subreddit as a platform to harass individuals when moderators don't take action," Reddit announced in a statement on the site. "We're banning behavior, not ideas." [32] Soon after, five communities that had repeatedly harassed people were banned.

These changes didn't go over well, to put it mildly: by the start of July, a revolt had begun, with thousands of moderators setting the subreddits they managed to "private," effectively blacking them out—a major blow to Reddit's advertising revenue. Many users blamed CEO Ellen Pao for the crackdowns, barraging her with racist and misogynist messages. A few days later, she resigned.

So how did a site that's used by so many people—one of the most popular sites on the entire web—not just become a haven for awful content, but create a large, vocal community that would revolt against removing that content? Observing the situation from the outside, wrote Jeong at the time, "it looks like a form of collective insanity, a sign that Reddit itself is overrun with the denizens of r/CoonTown, utterly broken beyond repair. . . . How can such a mainstream site appear to be so fringe?" [33]

But the answer isn't that most Reddit users want a site overrun with racist bile and violent sexism. It's that, like Twitter, the very feature that allowed Reddit to grow is the one that makes the harassment problem impossible to fix: the subreddit.

Each subreddit has one or more moderators—people who set ground rules for forum participants and are responsible for weeding out posts that don't comply. Reddit itself stays hands-off. Reddit has long touted this approach as being the ideal way to let a community thrive: In a 2014 interview, Erik Martin, Reddit's first community manager and then the company's general manager, said, "We try to give them tools to customize their subreddits but to be honest, most of the tools made for moderators were made by other moderators. The community creates what it needs." [34]

Martin saw this hands-off approach as a fundamental strategy for Reddit: "Make the users do the hard part," [35] he once said. But moderators aren't paid Reddit employees; they're volunteers. And by the time Reddit changed its policy in 2015, many of those volunteers had decided that the part Reddit required them to play had become *too* hard.

Back in August of 2014, just after Mike Brown was shot by police and Ferguson, Missouri, erupted into protests, the subreddit r/blackladies, a community for black women, was inundated with hateful, racist posts. "The moderators . . . tried to delete the hateful content as best they could, but the entire experience exhausted and demoralized them," wrote Aaron Sankin in the *Daily Dot*. "They contacted Reddit's management, but were told that, because the trolls weren't technically breaking any of the site's core rules, there was . . . nothing Reddit would do about it." [36]

When management rejected their requests for help, the moderators published an open letter on the r/blackladies subreddit, demanding that the problem be addressed. "Moderators volunteer to protect the community, and the constant vigilance required to do so takes an unnecessary toll," they wrote. "We need a proactive solution for this threat to our well-being. . . . We are here, we do not want to be hidden, and we do not want to be pushed away." [37] More than seventy other subreddit moderators cosigned the post.

You might think these moderators would have been pleased, then, about the changes in policy in 2015. But the problem was that, despite the new policies, Reddit still saw its role as fundamentally hands-off: moderators were the ones responsible for enforcing the new rules. As Jeong put it, what's breaking Reddit is "the same cost-efficient model that made it rise to the top." [38] She wrote:

> Reddit's supposed commitment to free speech is actually a punting of responsibility. It is expensive for Reddit to make and maintain the rules that would keep subreddits orderly, on-topic and not full of garbage (or at least, not hopelessly full of garbage). Only by giving their moderators near absolute power (under the guise of "free speech") can Reddit exist in the first place. [39]

As I write this, Reddit's moderation problems continue. At the start of February 2017, the site banned two subreddits run by the alt-right movement—ostensibly not for their terrifying hate speech (of which there was plenty), but rather because they violated a core tenet of the site, one of the only guiding principles it has: no doxing. That is, users can't release the "documents"—anything with personally identifiable information—of another person. [40] Just two days earlier, though, Reddit cofounder Ohanian had written an open letter condemning President Trump's executive order on immigration, and sharing the story of his own immigrant family. [41] Many users connected that post with the alt-right ban and accused Ohanian of politicizing the platform. Whether the timing was coincidental doesn't really matter: as long as Reddit maintains a "free speech" ideology that relies on unpaid moderators to function, it will continue to fall apart—and the victims will be those on the receiving end of harassment.

FAKING NEWS

Speaking of broken platforms and the American president, I would be remiss not to talk about perhaps the biggest story related to technology and the 2016 election: "fake news." As I write this today, the term has pretty much lost its meaning: the president and his staff now use it to vilify any press coverage they don't like. But during the fall of 2016, actual fake news was all over Facebook: *The Pope endorses Donald Trump! Hillary Clinton sold weapons to ISIS!*

According to a *BuzzFeed News* analysis, in the run-up to Election Day 2016, the top twenty fake stories from hoax and hyperpartisan sources generated more engagement on Facebook than the top twenty election stories from major news sites: 8.7 million shares, comments, and reactions, versus 7.4 million from real news sources.[42]

Most reports traced the problem back to May of 2016, when tech news site *Gizmodo* published an article based on an interview with former members of Facebook's Trending team. One of those staffers claimed that the small group of curators—editors who worked for Facebook on contract through third-party recruiting firms—had been biased against conservative news, routinely preventing topics like "Rand Paul" or "Glenn Beck" from appearing in the "Trending" section in the top-right corner of users' Facebook pages.[43] Political pundits went wild, and pretty soon, Senator John Thune of South Dakota—a ranking Republican—was demanding that Facebook explain itself to the Committee on Commerce, Science, and Transportation, where he was chair.[44]

These curators hadn't always existed. In 2014, when Facebook launched the Trending feature, an algorithm decided which stories made the cut. But, as at Reddit, the Ferguson protests turned out to be a lightning rod: while #blacklivesmatter and #ferguson lit up Twitter for days, Facebook's Trending section was full of those feel-good Ice Bucket Challenge videos. Facebook, which had been making a play to be seen as a credible news source, didn't like being criticized for missing the country's biggest news story at the time, so it decided to bring in some humans to help curate the news. That's how the team that *Gizmodo* profiled in 2016 came to be.

In the wake of the allegations, Facebook launched its own investigation, finding "no evidence of systemic bias." But it didn't matter: in August, the Trending team was suddenly laid off, and a group of engineers took its place to monitor the performance of the Trending algorithm.[45] Within three days, that algorithm was pushing fake news to the top of the feed: "BREAKING: Fox News Exposes Traitor Megyn Kelly, Kicks Her Out for Backing Hillary," the headline read. The story was fake, its description was riddled with typos, and the site it appeared on was anything but credible: EndingTheFed.com, run by a twenty-four-year-old Romanian man who copied and pasted stories from other conservative-leaning fake-news sites. Yet the story stayed at the top of the Trending charts for hours. Four different stories from EndingTheFed.com went on to make it into *BuzzFeed*'s list of most-shared fake-news articles during the election.[46] This time, conservative pundits and politicians were silent.

You might think this whole episode was a blunder: Facebook was put under pressure and made a rash decision, and fake news was the unintended consequence. But the truth about Trending isn't so straightforward. Former curators told *Gizmodo* that, after working there for a while, they realized they hadn't really been hired to be journalists. They were meant to "serve as training modules for Facebook's algorithm." While there, they were also told not to mention publicly that they were working for Facebook. "I got the sense that they wanted to keep the magic about how trending topics work a secret," one said. "We had to write in the most passive tense possible. That's why you'd see headlines that appear in an alien-esque, passive language." [47]

While the curators kept Trending's headlines faceless and machinelike, engineers were working behind the scenes, tweaking the machines themselves—the algorithms powering the feed of topics that the curators were responsible for picking through. Only, the curators had no direct contact with the engineers—no way to give them feedback on the system, or to confirm whether the machine was getting better or worse.

After the bias allegations, Facebook started testing a new version of Trending, one that replaced curator-written summaries with a simple number denoting how many people were talking about that topic. It also took away editors' ability to change the source associated with a topic. For example, if the algorithm selected Ending the Fed's story among several on the same topic—including, say, stories by Fox News or CNN—the editors had no way of shifting the Trending link to one of the other sources.

The tests, with both internal staff and small, randomly selected groups of public users, didn't go well. "The feedback they got internally was overwhelmingly negative. People would say, 'I don't understand why I'm looking at this. I don't see the context anymore.' There were spelling mistakes in the headlines. And the number of people talking about a topic would just be wildly off," a former curator told *Slate*. The curators expected the new version to be pulled and improved. Instead, they lost their jobs—and that botched version went to the public.[48]

In other words, Facebook did precisely what it had always intended with Trending: it made it machine-driven. The human phase of the operation just ended more quickly than expected. And when we look closer at Facebook's history, we can see that this wasn't a surprising choice at all. It's right in line with the values the company has always held.

When Facebook launched as a website for college students, back in 2004, users didn't have "feeds." They had profile pages. If you wanted to see what people were up to, you'd go to their "wall" and see what was on it; the content wouldn't come to you. In 2006, the introduction of the News Feed changed that: when you logged into Facebook, you'd get a stream of the latest actions your friends had taken there, like posting a photo, joining a group, or writing a status update. As the site grew more popular, people's networks got bigger—big enough that people couldn't keep up with everything in their feed anymore. Over time, Facebook started moving away from the reverse-chronological News Feed, and started moving to an algorithmically ordered one instead. Rather than seeing all your friends' posts, you then saw the ones Facebook decided were the most relevant to you. "Our whole mission is to show people content that we think that they find meaningful," said Adam Mosseri, Facebook's vice president of product management, in a 2015 interview with *Time*. "Recency is one important input into what people find meaningful, but we have found over and over again that it's not the only one."[49]

At this point, most of us accept the News Feed algorithm, even if we don't quite know what it's doing. That's just how Facebook works. But it didn't *have* to be how Facebook works: users could have been given more power to choose whose posts they saw most, or to keep their profiles chronological. They could have been allowed to split their feed into multiple views, for different topics. They could have been given filter options, such as choosing to see only original posts, not shared content. There are many, many ways Facebook could have solved the problem of people having more content in their feed than they could keep up with. But rather than solving it with more user control, more human influence, they solved it with machines.

The same is true about the allegations of bias on the Trending team: according to *Gizmodo*'s report, the people involved were nearly all in their twenties and early thirties, and had attended primarily Ivy League colleges or other elite East Coast schools. Most of them leaned liberal. If Facebook was concerned about bias, it could have filled these roles with a more diverse team—people from a variety of backgrounds, ages, and, yes, political leanings. It could have updated the list of news publications that editors relied on to decide whether something was a national story. It could have adjusted editorial oversight. Hell, it could have made the news curators part of the product team, and involved them in the process of improving the algorithm.

But instead, Facebook once again decided to just let the machines sort it out, and pick up the pieces later. Only this time, there was a lot more at stake than users missing a few photos from their favorite friends, or seeing too many updates from a friend's cousin who they hung out with once at a wedding.

These core values aren't new. In fact, if you ask Mark Zuckerberg, they're the core of the company, and always have been. Back when Facebook filed for IPO, in 2012, he lauded those values in a letter to investors: "As most companies grow, they slow down too much because they're more afraid of making mistakes than they are of losing opportunities by moving too slowly," he wrote. "We have a saying: 'Move fast and break things.' The idea is that if you never break anything, you're probably not moving fast enough." [50]

Zuckerberg famously calls this approach "the Hacker Way": build something quickly, release it to the world, see what happens, and then make adjustments. The idea is so ingrained in Facebook's culture—so core to the way it sees the world—that One Hacker Way is even the official address of the company's fancy Menlo Park headquarters.

That's why it was so easy for fake news to take hold on Facebook: combine the deeply held conviction that you can engineer your way out of anything with a culture focused on moving fast without worrying about the implications, and you don't just break *things*. You break public access to information. You break trust. You break *people*.

Facebook didn't *mean* to make fake news a real problem, just like Twitter didn't *mean* to enable harassers. But Facebook's unquestioning commitment to the Hacker Way—to a belief system that puts technical solutions first, and encourages programmers and product teams to take risks without thinking about their implications—made it easy for it to stay blind to the problem, until it was far too late.

The bigger Facebook's ambitions get, the riskier these cultural values become. It's one thing to play fast and loose with people's cat photos and status updates. It's another when you start proclaiming that you're "developing the social infrastructure for community—for supporting us, for keeping us safe, for informing us, for civic engagement, and for inclusion of all," as Zuckerberg himself wrote in a 5,000-word manifesto about the future of the company published in February 2017.[51] He went on to talk about a future where Facebook AI listens in on conversations to identify potential terrorists, where elected officials hold meetings on Facebook, and where a "global safety infrastructure" responds to emergencies ranging from disease outbreaks to natural disasters to refugee crises.

Are we comfortable leaving all this to a tech company—one that's still run mostly by white guys from California, and where the people who actually have professional experience informing the public don't even get to talk to the engineers who train machines to take their jobs? If we want a world that works for everyone—not just acolytes of the Hacker Way—we shouldn't be.

SLOW DOWN AND FIX STUFF

The platforms in this chapter have much in common: they rose to power during the early 2000s, and built unique models of social connection. They also share an abdication of responsibility—a collective shrug of the shoulders at the harm they have caused, and an unwillingness to take responsibility for preventing it in the future.

That worldview simply doesn't match the effect their platforms have on users—and, because of those platforms' reach, on the world at large. According to Caterina Fake, the cofounder of photo-sharing site Flickr and recommendation product Hunch, "A lot of people, when they build software, believe that they have written the code and then are done." But, she told the podcast *Note to Self,* that's a delusion. "That is where the problems begin, because that is the starting point. Without all the work that goes into creating a civilized society online, it devolves." [52] Fake suggests that the tech industry instead needs to stop prioritizing programming over every other skill. Rather than relegate people with editorial and ethical judgment to the basement (which is literally where Facebook housed its curators), it needs a "conscious approach," where ethics, media literacy, and historical context are taken into account.

That's the problem with the platforms we rely on today. It's not just that these tech companies lack diverse staffs (though they certainly do). It's that the founders believe so deeply in their own vision—and have been rewarded for it for so long—that they don't realize how narrow that vision is, and how many humans it could harm. They don't realize they need people around them with different perspectives, because they've never considered the limitations of their own perspectives in the first place. After all, in a world where machines can fix everything, it doesn't matter what you break. If you're blind to the consequences, good intentions seem good enough. And the rest of us pay the price.

Chapter 9

Meritocracy Now, Meritocracy Forever

Biased algorithms. Alienating online forms. Harassment-friendly platforms. All kinds of problems plague digital products, from tiny design details to massively flawed features. But they share a common foundation: a tech culture that's built on white, male values—while insisting it's brilliant enough to serve all of us.

Or, as they call it in Silicon Valley, "meritocracy."

It's a term you'll hear constantly in tech, whether in a Hacker News forum or on Twitter or in line for coffee in San Francisco. The argument is simple: the tech industry is based purely on merit, and the people who are at the top got there because they were smarter, more innovative, and more ambitious than everyone else. If a company doesn't employ many women or people of color—well, it's just because no good ones applied. After all, the story goes, "Silicon Valley is swimming in money"[1]—so, clearly nothing's wrong (never mind that by these criteria alone, you can justify everything from the heroin trade to chattel slavery).

The funny thing about meritocracy is that the concept comes not from any coherent political ideology or sociological research. It comes from satire. In 1958, sociologist Michael Young wrote a book lampooning the then-stratified British education system. In it, he depicts a dystopian future where IQ testing defines citizens' educational options and, eventually, their entire lives—dividing the country into an elite ruling class of "merited" people, and an underclass of those without merit. The public loved the word, but lost the point. Almost immediately, the term "meritocracy" was cropping up in a positive light—particularly in the United States (we've never been great at detecting British sarcasm).

Young didn't take kindly to the public's positive adoption of his word. "I have been sadly disappointed by my 1958 book," he wrote in the *Guardian* in 2001, shortly before he died. "The book was a satire meant to be a warning (which needless to say has not been heeded)." [2]

If he was frustrated then, he must be rolling in his grave now. Venture capitalists routinely fund startups run by white guys because they share the same background as a past success—not because they have more merit. According to a 2013 *Reuters* analysis, of eighty-eight tech companies that received "Series A" funding from one of the five top Silicon Valley venture firms between the start of 2011 and June of 2013, seventy of them—80 percent—had founders from what *Reuters* dubbed the "traditional Silicon Valley cohort": people who'd already started a successful company in the past; who worked in the industry already, either in a senior role at a large tech company or at a well-connected smaller one; or who attended one of three elite colleges: MIT, Stanford, or Harvard.

Startup success, *Reuters* writer Sarah McBride concluded, wasn't actually much different from success in other elite professions. "A prestigious degree, a proven track record and personal connections to power-brokers are at least as important as a great idea," she wrote. "Scrappy unknowns with a suitcase and a dream are the exceptions, not the rule." [3] As Sharon Vosmek, CEO of the venture accelerator Astia, put it, "They call it pattern recognition, but in other industries they call it profiling or stereotyping." [4] Meanwhile, women hardly get funded at all: only 10 percent of the 187 Silicon Valley startups that received Series A funding in 2016 were woman-led, up a meager 2 percent from the year before. [5]

Yet much of the tech industry still clings to meritocracy like a tattered baby blanket. Sequoia Capital partner Greg McAdoo insisted, "This business is a meritocracy by and large." [6] David Sacks, an early executive at PayPal, claimed that "if meritocracy exists anywhere on earth, it is in Silicon Valley." [7] Until 2014, code-hosting platform GitHub even put a rug emblazoned with "United Meritocracy of GitHub" in the center of its Oval Office–replica waiting room. [8] In the fall of 2016, the *Atlantic* sent out its annual "pulse of the technology industry" survey to influential executives, founders, and thinkers—and found that "men were three times as likely as women to say Silicon Valley is a meritocracy." [9]

It's not just tech that wants desperately to believe in a meritocracy, of course. American culture has always promulgated the myth of the self-made man—the Horatio Alger character who pulls himself up by his bootstraps. But the meritocracy myth is particularly pernicious in tech, because it encourages the belief that the industry doesn't need to listen to outside voices— because the smartest people are always already in the room. This presumption quickly breeds a sort of techno-paternalism: when a group of mostly white guys from mostly the same places believes it deserves to be at the top, it's also quick to assume that it has all the perspective it needs in order to make decisions for everyone else.

Tied up in this meritocracy myth is also the assumption that technical skills are the most difficult to learn—and that if people study something else, it's because they couldn't hack programming. As a result, the system prizes technical abilities—and systematically devalues the people who bring the very skills to the table that could strengthen products, both ethically and commercially: people with the humanities and social science training needed to consider historical and cultural context, identify unconscious bias, and be more empathetic to the needs of users.

We need that kind of perspective now more than ever. Tech has become both a driving force in the economy and a mediator of almost every experience you can imagine. And, more and more, those experiences aren't driven solely by human choices, but by decisions made by machines. This means the biases and blind spots that tech perpetuates aren't just worming their way into individual hearts and minds, but literally becoming embedded in infrastructures that humans can't easily see, much less critically assess or fix. Because, as we saw in Chapter 7, once an algorithm learns that women are homemakers, or that black people are criminals, the bias sticks around—long after we realize it's there.

So let's look more closely at how clinging to meritocracy myths can turn a tech company toxic, why doing so keeps the industry from becoming more representative, and what happens when an organization decides to do things differently.

THE MERITOCRACY MELTDOWN

On a fall day in 2015, Susan Fowler showed up for her first day of work as a site reliability engineer at Uber. She was thrilled: her department was new, her coworkers were smart, and she was told she could join any project she wanted. She spent a couple weeks in training, and then joined an engineering team that focused on her area of expertise.

Her first day on the team, everything changed: her direct manager propositioned her for sex over chat. She reported the incident to human resources immediately, with screenshots of the conversation.

Then things got worse. HR reps told her that her manager, a "top performer," had never been accused before, so they weren't comfortable punishing him with anything more than a warning. She could either stay on his team—the team where her expertise was most valuable—or find a new one in the organization to switch to. But if she stayed, they warned, her manager would probably give her a bad review, and there was nothing they could do about it. Upper management didn't help: they told her they didn't want to ruin his career.

Fowler felt she had no choice. She found another team. Pretty soon, she also found other women engineers who told her they'd been harassed by the same manager and been told the same story: that he was a high performer, that it was his first time being accused, and that they would talk to him. Meeting after meeting with HR and management went nowhere.

For the next year, Fowler was in hell: she was subjected to sexist comments; threatened that she should not communicate with other women staff members about her experiences; and told that, despite her stellar performance reviews, she had "undocumented performance problems" that prevented her from changing teams. By the end of 2016, she'd had enough. She quit, leaving for the online payment company Stripe instead.

One Sunday the following February, she decided to tell her story. She published a painstakingly detailed, 3,000-word post to her personal blog outlining precisely what had happened.[10] The internet went wild. That same day, CEO Travis Kalanick released a statement calling Fowler's experience "abhorrent and against everything Uber stands for and believes in,"[11] and claiming this was the first he'd heard of the problem. By Monday, he'd hired former attorney general Eric Holder's law firm to investigate sexual harassment at the company, and he said that investor Arianna Huffington and others would be reviewing findings shortly.[12] Within days, two more stories of sexual harassment and humiliation at Uber had been published, and countless others confirmed that the company culture was as they described it: aggressive, degrading, and chaotic. In the middle of the mess, a new hire—Amit Singhal, Uber's vice president of engineering—resigned, after reports surfaced that he'd been pushed out of Google a year before because of sexual harassment allegations.[13]

It wasn't the first PR disaster, or the last, to send the ride-hailing company into a tailspin in the first months of 2017. Just weeks earlier, *Bloomberg* had published a feature story on Uber drivers who couldn't afford housing and spent most nights sleeping in their cars.[14] In late January, Kalanick had gotten heat for joining President Trump's advisory council. Then, the company sent cars to JFK airport, where NYC taxi drivers were boycotting in protest of Trump's executive order barring legal immigrants of seven countries from entering the United States. Critics saw the move as profiteering, and started a campaign: #deleteuber.[15] Within days, more than 200,000 people had done just that.[16] Soon after, Kalanick resigned from Trump's council.

Then, just nine days after Fowler's story was published, a leaked dashboard video of Kalanick arguing with an Uber driver went viral. In the video, Kalanick gets in the car with two women and makes small talk. One mentions that she's heard it's been a hard year at Uber. "I make sure every year is a hard year," he tells her. "That's kind of how I roll." Before leaving, he mentions to the driver that changes to the "black car" system are coming. The driver says he knows and is concerned that Uber is dropping rates for drivers. Pretty soon, Kalanick is screaming at the man. "Bullshit! Bullshit!" he yells. "You know what, some people don't like to take responsibility for their own shit. They blame everything in their life on somebody else." [17] It wasn't a good look.

Kalanick's public apology was swift. The very next day, he said he was "ashamed" of his behavior. "I must fundamentally change as a leader and grow up," he wrote.[18]

This wasn't a one-off event for Kalanick, but rather par for the awful course. He had once told *GQ* that Uber's success got him women on demand, quipping, "We call that Boob-er." [19] When a woman reported being strangled by her driver, Kalanick blamed the media for making Uber "somehow liable for these incidents that aren't even real in the first place." [20]

So, what allows a forty-year-old man to avoid "growing up" for so long, even while commanding a company that was, as of this writing, last valuated at $68 billion? It's our friend the "meritocracy," of course.

At Uber, meritocracy isn't just an informal belief, but is actually enshrined in its fourteen core values—standards the company expects everyone on staff to live by: "meritocracy and toe-stepping," it reads, alongside such visionary statements as "always be hustlin'" and "superpumped." [21] (Don't worry, no one really knows what they mean.)

The problem is that Uber's idea of meritocracy—a workplace where the best idea wins, and people are encouraged to clamber over one another to have their name on it—tends to fall back on a really narrow concept of "best." Take the harassment charges levied by "Amy," a self-proclaimed "Uber survivor" who published her experiences in an anonymous post on Medium just after Fowler went public (and whose story Uber said would be forwarded to Holder's investigation team as well). Among her list of harrowing events—which included high-ranking men talking about her ass and colleagues nicknaming an Asian team member "slanty-eyed Joe"—was this gem: A senior male colleague proposed an idea to block a driver's payment if a customer complained. "I told them that it was unethical to block a driver's payments without researching the complaint to make sure it was the driver's fault," she wrote, noting that many drivers live in countries where they do not own their cars and hand over their wages to another party. Blocking payments could leave them without income. "There is no place for ethics in this business sweetheart. We are not a charity," she recalls the senior manager responding. When she persisted, he covered the microphone on their conference call line, grabbed her hand, and told her to "stop being a whiny little bitch."[22]

Stories like these are why I laugh whenever someone mentions improving the "pipeline" of diverse students graduating with tech industry-ready skills: Why? So we can get more women and people of color into a field that's going to chew them up and spit them out, all while telling them to smile more or making their ethnicity the butt of jokes? So we can tell more of them to speak up in meetings—while never acknowledging the fact that speaking up is often what leads them to be seen as "abrasive" or "difficult"?

PIPELINE TO NOWHERE

Of course, the tech industry *does* have pipeline problems: colleges are graduating relatively few women with computer science degrees, and even fewer black and Hispanic students. For example, the most recent numbers from the National Science Foundation (NSF), from 2014, reported that just 18 percent of computer science bachelor's degrees went to women.[23]

What's interesting about these NSF numbers, though, is that comparing stats over time reveals that women are actually earning *fewer* degrees in computer science, not more. Originally, programming was often categorized as "women's work," lumped in with administrative skills like typing and dictation (in fact, during World War II, the word "computers" was often applied not to machines, but to the women who used them to compute data). As more colleges started offering computer science degrees, in the 1960s, women flocked to the programs: 11 percent of computer science majors in 1967 were women. By 1984, that number had grown to 37 percent. Starting in 1985, that percentage fell every single year—until, in 2007, it leveled out at the 18 percent figure we saw through 2014.

That shift coincides perfectly with the rise of the personal computer—which was marketed almost exclusively to men and boys.[24] We heard endless stories about Steve Jobs, Bill Gates, Paul Allen—garage tinkerers, boy geniuses, *geeks*. Software companies, and soon after, internet companies, all showcased men at the helm, backed by a sea of techies who looked just like them.

And along the way, women stopped studying computer science, even as more of them were attending college than ever before.

I can't pretend to know the precise reasons for this shift, but if people can't imagine themselves working in a field, then they won't study it. And it's hard to imagine yourself fitting into a profession where you can't see anyone who looks like you.

That's why it's critical that tech companies not just recruit diverse staff, but also work their asses off to keep them. Because unless tech can showcase all kinds of people thriving in its culture, women and underrepresented groups will continue to major in something else—something they can imagine fitting into. In other words, blame the pipeline all you want, but diverse people won't close their eyes and jump in until they know it'll be a safe place for them when they get to the other side. No matter how many black girls you send to code camp.

Today, though, tech companies struggle mightily to retain the women and underrepresented minorities they *do* manage to hire. In a 2008 study that included thousands of women working in the private sector in science, engineering, and technology (SET, which, I should note, includes a range of fields broader than just web and software development), researchers found that more than half the women quit their jobs, "driven out by hostile work environments and extreme job pressures."[25] Another found that nearly one-third of women in SET positions felt stalled in their careers—and for black women, that number shot up to almost half.[26]

You might assume that much of the attrition comes from women leaving to start or care for a family. Nope. Only about 20 percent of those who quit SET leave the workforce. The rest either take their technical skills to another industry (working for a nonprofit or in education, say), or move to a nontechnical position.

People call this the "leaky bucket": when women and under-represented groups leave because they're fed up with biased cultures where they can't get ahead. No pipeline in the world can make up for a steady flow out of tech companies. Cate Huston, the mobile lead for Automattic (the company behind WordPress) and a prominent programmer, has even gone so far as to assume she's headed in that direction herself, and says her colleagues feel the same:

We joke about it, other women and I, what we will finally do when we leave. Become a barista. Go back to school. "Pull a disappearing act," one friend says, leaving it to me to explain the chaos she left behind. "Not if I get there first," I reply.[27]

And so the cycle continues: tech sends out another round of press releases detailing meager increases in diversity and calling for more programs to teach middle schoolers to code, and another generation of women and people of color in tech pushes to be visible and valued in an industry that wants diversity *numbers*, but doesn't want to disrupt its culture to get or keep diverse *people*.

A LOSING PROPOSITION

Now, I happen to care about all this because I care about people. I want anyone with skills and ideas to be able to enter one of the biggest, richest, most promising sectors of the economy without enduring harassment or years of unequal pay or the relentless suspicion of coworkers who think that they got their job only because of "quotas." But I know someone's got their fingers perched on the caps-lock key right now, ready to send me a scathing email about how tech companies aren't charities, and demanding to know why diversity matters to "THE BOT-TOM LINE."

I'll probably get that email no matter what I say next, but here's the truth: *Study after study shows that diverse teams perform better.*

In a 2014 report for *Scientific American,* Columbia professor Katherine W. Phillips examined a broad cross section of research related to diversity and organizational performance. And over and over, she found that the simple act of interacting in a diverse group improves performance, because it "forces group members to prepare better, to anticipate alternative viewpoints and to expect that reaching consensus will take effort." [28]

In one study that Phillips cited, published in the *Journal of Personal Social Psychology,* researchers asked participants to serve on a mock jury for a black defendant. Some participants were assigned to diverse juries, some to homogenous ones. Across the board, diverse groups were more careful with details than were homogenous groups, and more open to conversation. When white participants were in diverse groups rather than homogenous ones, they were more likely to cite facts (rather than opinions), and they made fewer errors, the study found. "Even before discussion, Whites in diverse groups were more lenient toward the Black defendant, demonstrating that the effects of diversity do not occur solely through information exchange." [29]

In another study, led by Phillips and researchers from Stanford and the University of Illinois at Urbana-Champaign, undergraduate students from the University of Illinois were asked to participate in a murder-mystery exercise. Each student was assigned to a group of three, with some groups composed of two white students and one nonwhite student, and some composed of three white students. Each group member was given both a common set of information and a set of unique clues that the other members did not have. Group members needed to share all the information they collectively possessed in order to solve the puzzle. But students in all-white groups were significantly less likely to do so, and therefore performed significantly worse in the exercise. The reason is that when we work only with those similar to us, we often "think we all hold the same information and share the same perspective," Phillips writes. "This perspective, which stopped the all-white groups from effectively processing the information, is what hinders creativity and innovation." [30]

But does any of this affect companies' finances? Some research indicates so. In another study that Phillips reviewed, business professors Cristian Deszö of the University of Maryland and David Ross of Columbia wanted to understand how gender representation in top firms correlated with those firms' performance. They reviewed the size and gender composition of senior management teams across the Standard & Poor's Composite 1500 list, and then compared that information with financial data. What they found was staggering: "Female representation in top management leads to an increase of $42 million in firm value," they wrote.[31] In addition, they found that firms with a higher "innovation intensity," measured as the ratio of research and development expenses to assets, were more successful financially when top leadership included women.

Meanwhile, a 2003 study of 177 national banks in the United States compared "financial performance, racial diversity and the emphasis the bank presidents put on innovation." In that study, Phillips reports, "for innovation-focused banks, increases in racial diversity were clearly related to enhanced financial performance."[32]

SPECIAL RULES FOR SPECIAL PEOPLE

The tech industry knows it has a diversity problem. It knows that diverse teams perform better. It also knows it needs programmers and designers—badly enough to pay six-figure starting salaries to twenty-two-year-old computer science graduates. Why, then, aren't things getting better, faster? How can the industry that put a powerful computer in my pocket and self-driving cars on the street not be able to figure out how to get more diverse candidates into its companies?

Well, I'll tell you the secret. It's because tech doesn't really want to—or at least, not as much as it wants something else: lack of oversight.

Consider the entire concept of the "tech industry." As Anil Dash puts it, everything from subprime auto leasing (through Uber) to mayonnaise (Hampton Creek's Just Mayo) to medical testing (the now-discredited Theranos) has been lumped under this single umbrella, and funded by Silicon Valley investors:

> Absurdly, we're expecting lawmakers, the media and aver-
> age consumers to understand these wildly different offer-
> ings . . . as part of one single, endlessly complex, industry.
> That's an impossible task. . . . Perpetuating the myth of a
> monolithic "tech industry" overtaxes our ability to man-
> age the changes that technology is making to society.[33]

Dash concludes that, ultimately, the tech industry doesn't really exist. It's just in these organizations' best interests to be seen as "tech." Take Uber: If it were perceived as a taxi service, or an auto loan financer, it would be part of an industry with existing regulations and expectations (even if those industries have problems, which, well, yeah). But by being labeled "technology"—by being better known as an app you download to your phone, rather than a massively complex system of vehicles and drivers—Uber gets to change the conversation. Instead of discussing the ethics of hiring legions of drivers as "independent contractors" and then selling them high-interest subprime loans to finance the vehicles they need to do their jobs (while aggressively pursuing the driverless technologies that will take away all those jobs), you're encouraged to marvel at the seamlessness of the experience as you watch a little car icon navigate the streets on its way to your location. Uber's not a taxi company. It's *superpumped*. It's special.

In other words, Uber's product isn't full of oversights. It's not making mistakes. It just doesn't care, and it doesn't think it should have to. As the *Verge* put it, "Uber's problems didn't just materialize out of the blue this past January. Uber has been burning through capital, pissing off drivers, alienating riders, and generally wreaking havoc since its inception over six years ago," they wrote. "It's shady business—even for a business with a reputation for shadiness." [34]

Uber may be an extreme example, but it can help us understand tech's insular culture much more clearly: if tech wants to be seen as special—and therefore able to operate outside the rules—then it helps to position the people working inside tech companies as special too. And the best way to ensure that happens is to build a monoculture, where insiders bond over a shared belief in their own brilliance. That's also why you see so many ridiculous job titles floating around Silicon Valley and places like it: "rock-star" designers, "ninja" JavaScript developers, user-experience "unicorns" (yes, these are all real). Fantastical labels like these reinforce the idea that tech and design are magical: skill sets that those on the outside wouldn't understand, and could never learn.

The reality is a lot more mundane: design and programming are just professions—sets of skills and practices, just like any other field. Admitting that truth would make tech positions feel a lot more welcoming to diverse employees, but tech can't tell that story to the masses. If it did, then the industry would seem normal, understandable, and accessible—and that would make everyday people more comfortable pushing back when its ideas are intrusive or unethical. So, tech has to maintain its insider-y, more-brilliant-than-thou feel—which affects who decides to enter that legendary "pipeline," and whether they'll stick around once they've arrived.

Plus, there's the pesky problem of how diverse teams challenge existing cultures. In all that research about the benefits of diversity, one finding sticks out: it can feel harder to work on a diverse team. "Dealing with outsiders causes friction, which feels counterproductive," write researchers David Rock, Heidi Grant, and Jacqui Grey.[35] But experiments have shown that this type of friction is actually helpful, because it leads teams to push past easy answers and think through solutions more carefully. "In fact, working on diverse teams produces better outcomes precisely *because* it's harder," they conclude. That's a tough sell for tech companies, though. As soon as you invite in "outsiders" who question the status quo—people like Uber's "Amy," who ask whether the choices being made are ethical—it's hard to skate by without scrutiny anymore. As a result, maintaining the monoculture becomes more important than improving products.

REJECTING THE MYTH

Not every tech company looks at the world like Uber does (thank god). Just look at messaging app Slack, a darling of the startup world with an office motto that's refreshingly healthy: "Work hard and go home."[36]

Meanwhile, Slack is a product people love—in a way no one expects to love business software. It's often described as a delight to use—but it's a delight borne of nuance and detail, not shoved-down-your-throat cuteness. And the company got there by what so few tech companies seem to bother with: considering their users as real, whole people. CEO Stewart Butterfield reportedly even asks designers to close their eyes and imagine what a person might have experienced in their life before sitting down at their desk. "Maybe they were running late and sat in gridlock for an hour. Maybe they had an argument with their spouse. Maybe they're stressed out. The last thing they need is to struggle with a computer program that seems intent on making their day worse." [37]

As a result, the product is more respectful than most any other messaging system: There are endless ways to customize Slack to your day, such as snoozing notifications in the evening, or turning off notifications for things you don't care about. You can easily mute sound effects. And the little bits of copy that guide you around the interface or alert you to new features are witty, but never at your expense.

The care extends to hiring as well. One of the first things Butterfield wants to know about when interviewing candidates for a position isn't which programming languages they know or where their computer science degree is from. It's whether they believe luck played a role in getting them where they are—whether they think their success is a product not just of merit and talent, but of good circumstances. His goal is simple: to build a team where people *don't* assume they're special. No rock stars, no gurus, no ninjas—just people who bring a combination of expertise, humility, and empathy.

Lo and behold, that culture also leads to a more diverse staff: women held more than 40 percent of Slack's management positions in 2016, and more than a fourth of engineering roles too. Black people accounted for nearly 8 percent of engineers.[38] In fact, it's where Kaya Thomas, the black computer science student we met way back in Chapter 2, accepted an offer for her first postgraduation job.

Slack's disarming honesty and disinterest in chest thumping are antithetical to the way most of tech talks about itself. And it's working: Slack is the fastest-growing business app ever. It tripled its daily active user base in the first half of 2016 alone, from 1 million to 3 million, and grew its total paid accounts to almost 1 million. By October of that year, paid accounts had grown by another 33 percent, to 1.25 million.[39]

And no one had to sleep in their cars, or get coerced into a subprime auto loan, to do it.

DISRUPTING TECH CULTURE

What Slack has done is still small—just one company, just a few hundred employees. And I'm sure it's far from perfect there. But it's a powerful model that we should all be paying more attention to—because it upends tech's culture of mystification and exceptionalism. It doesn't rely on believing that programmers are the chosen ones (in fact, Butterfield, who has a master's degree in philosophy, is known for extolling the values of the liberal arts to anyone in tech who'll listen). It proves that there's no reason nice people making thoughtful choices can't produce tech products that are successful and profitable.

It proves that we can, in fact, expect more.

Pair Slack's story with Uber's bout of PR crises. If you ask me, Uber's bad press is just the first wave of a coming tide against tech companies. This backlash can't come fast enough. Because the tech industry prides itself on talking about the industries it disrupts. Taxis, groceries, you name it. But it seems to forget that a synonym for "disruption" is "instability." And instability is what's coming, in the form of artificial intelligence eating millions more jobs. After all, "if you are driving for Uber, your employer's plan is to automate your job."[40]

But generic antitech backlash isn't going to save us from impending disruption—unless we're willing to put down our phones and stop web-enabling all our appliances. The only real way to hold tech accountable, and to rid it of its worst excesses, is to demand that it become accessible to everyday people—both in the way it designs its products, and in who can thrive in its offices. Because as long as tech is allowed to operate as a zero-sum game—a place where anything goes, as long as it leads to a big IPO and an eventual multibillion-dollar sale—companies like Uber will exist.

Conversely, the more we remind tech companies that real people use their products—the more we demand to be taken seriously, and push to be represented fairly within their systems— the more chance we have that they'll see their role for what it really is: one that profoundly affects lives, livelihoods, and communities. One that comes with responsibility, not just endless "hockey-stick growth" (the term startups love to use whenever numbers suddenly shoot up exponentially) and a big payout.

Today's tech culture still expects the world to fetishize it: to treat it like an exotic, enthralling beast. Why wouldn't it? That's what most press has done for the past two decades. "Founders and their publicists would have you believe that this is a world of pioneers and utopians, cowboy coders and hero programmers," proclaimed tech-industry worker by day and freelance journalist by night Anna Wiener in the *Atlantic*. But that kind of coverage—"buzzy and breathless" blog posts, puff pieces "zeroing in on the trappings, trends, and celebrities of the tech scene"— doesn't cut it anymore, because it exempts the industry's elite "from the scrutiny that their economic and political power should invite."[41]

That's where we all come in. We don't have to respond to tech with a bat of the eyelashes and a look of wonder. We can be more critical, and less complacent. Because tech culture isn't something that belongs just to the engineers and venture capitalists. It's ours too.

Chapter 10
Technically Dangerous

I'm writing this book at a weird moment in America—weird enough that I spent a lot of time wondering whether I should bother writing at all. Who cares about tech in the face of deportations, propaganda, the threat of a second Cold War? Shouldn't I be in the street protesting?

More than once, that's what I did: I threw down my draft, picked up a marker, and headed for the subway with a homemade sign. "The injustices are just too big to worry about all of tech's petty problems right now," I would think as I marched through the streets. But the more often I found myself out there, looking around at my chanting neighbors—immigrants, women, black people, trans people, sick people, and so many more who are already marginalized or made invisible in our society—the more I knew: alienating and biased technology doesn't matter less during this time of political upheaval. It matters all the more.

I don't know what the United States will look like by the time you read this book, and in fact I'm anxious it will look even bleaker than I can yet imagine. But whatever happens, it will still be profoundly impacted by technology. And that technology will still, by and large, be designed by people who don't look like most of this country.

The narrower those people's perspectives are—the more they design and code for people like themselves, and shrug off any responsibility for the outcome—the more easily inequality, insensitivity, and hate can thrive. That harms users on an individual level: the trans woman who feels alienated by binary gender selectors, the multiracial person who feels erased when they have to choose to express one part of their identity over another, the parent cruelly triggered while grieving the death of their child. But it's not just a problem of digital microaggressions, of slights and snubs that remind people that they don't belong or that their experiences don't matter. It's also the way they reinforce biases and embolden bad behavior in the rest of the population. Culture doesn't just inform technology and design. Technology and design also, increasingly, inform culture.

We hold technology in our pockets. We tell it our secrets. We rely on it to sustain relationships. It's the first thing many of us interact with in the morning, and the last thing we look at at night. Technology isn't just pervasive. It's personal.

But it's when things get personal that change is possible. In a 2009 Gallup poll, researchers found that respondents who said they knew a gay person were 40 percent more likely to think that same-sex relationships should be legal, and 64 percent more likely to think that gay marriage would not change society for the worse, than those who reported not knowing any gay people. The implication is clear: exposure to difference changes perspective, and increases tolerance.[1]

That's why it matters so much that marginalized groups are validated within our interfaces. Because if technology has the power to connect the world, as technologists so often proclaim, then it also has the power to make the world a more inclusive place, simply by building interfaces that reflect *all* its users. When the needs of trans people are made explicitly visible within an interface, everyone who uses that interface gets a subtle reminder that trans people exist. The more visible trans people are online, the more a part of our communities they become—and the harder it is for them to be treated like a bogeyman and subjected to "bathroom bills."

Inclusion also saves lives. In early 2017, researchers from Johns Hopkins and Harvard published a study analyzing more than 750,000 responses from the Youth Risk Behavior Surveillance System, an annual study conducted by the Centers for Disease Control and Prevention. The data, which was gathered from surveys that American high-school students completed between 1999 and 2015, revealed that after a state legalized same-sex marriage, as thirty-two states did between 2004 and 2015, its rate of teen suicide attempts dropped by an average of more than 7 percent. Among LGBTQ students, who report suicide attempts at a staggering four times the rate of straight students, the decrease was even larger: 14 percent fewer reported that they'd attempted suicide after gay marriage passed in their state than before. In the fifteen states that did not legalize same-sex marriage in that time frame, rates stayed the same. According to the study's authors, if this reduction holds true for all US students, we'll see 134,000 fewer teen suicide attempts per year, now that marriage equality is national law.[2]

The study wasn't designed to assign causation, so the authors

are careful to note that they can't say for sure whether the legal-
ization of gay marriage directly caused the decreases. But it certainly appears that way. "Stigma is one of the most frequently
hypothesized risk factors for explaining sexual orientation dis-
parities in suicide outcomes," wrote Mark L. Hatzenbuehler of
Columbia University in an editorial accompanying the study in
JAMA Pediatrics.[3] But most past research had focused on the
effects of "individual and interpersonal" stigmas, rather than
the "broader, structural forms of stigma" that this research
pointed to: laws and cultural norms.

Changing form fields won't change laws. But the more our
daily interactions and tasks happen in digital spaces, the more
power those spaces hold over cultural norms. Every form field,
every default setting, every push notification, affects people.
Every detail can add to the culture we want—can make people a
little safer, a little calmer, a little more hopeful.

• • •

I'm sitting in Yerba Buena Gardens, a park in the heart of San
Francisco's SoMa neighborhood. It's a Friday in early spring,
just after 5 p.m., and that quintessentially Californian golden
light is bouncing off the waterfall-style fountain in front of me.
Twentysomethings hop into Ubers headed for happy hours and
yoga classes. A trio plops down at a table outside the tea shop
next to me to talk about user engagement rates and daily active
users. Young men pour out of the Game Developers Conference
at the Moscone Center next door, lanyards still around their
necks, making plans for an evening out. Everything feels easy—if
you avoid looking at the woman with a stroller and a cardboard
sign on the corner, or the man sleeping in an alcove over on How-

ard Street, or the fact that all your friends are leaving this place because their salaries, even the ones inflated by tech jobs, just don't stack up in a city where people make cash offers at open houses and the average two-bedroom apartment rents for more than $5,000 a month.

About a mile southwest, at Uber's headquarters, another scandal is brewing: a tool called "Greyball," used to systematically mislead authorities in markets where the service was banned or under investigation, has just been reported in the *New York Times*.[4] Across the street, at Twitter, stock prices fell more than 10 percent in a single month, and the company is scrambling.[5] And thirty miles south, in Menlo Park, Facebook has just started rolling out its solution to fake news: stories shared on Facebook that have been debunked by third-party, nonpartisan fact-checking organizations have begun being marked with a red caution icon and the word "Disputed"—a label that's already being disputed itself, with some calling it censorship and others calling it too milquetoast for news that's demonstrably false.[6]

Unrest is brewing at the big tech companies. I don't feel bad for them. Tech has spent too long being treated as a marvel—getting a free pass on ethics by promising us convenience wrapped in a slickly designed package. It's time to turn on the pressure, and keep it on until things change. Send customer service complaints. Tell the media. Write your congressperson. Support an alternate product.

If we don't, there's real danger ahead. Tech companies are now engaging in all manner of civic life—from Mark Zuckerberg's vision for a journalism industry utterly intertwined with Facebook, to the downright terrifying work of Trump adviser Peter Thiel's data-mining company Palantir, which received $41 million from Immigration and Customs Enforcement to build software that tracks and deports immigrants (and could, of course, be turned on any of us).[7] If tech companies can't get the basics right—if they can't stop themselves from designing "yellowface" photo filters, or pushing cutesy language at people in crisis, or creating photo-tagging systems that fail black users— why should we trust them to provide solutions to massive societal problems?

We'll only be successful in ridding tech of its excesses and oversights if we first embrace a new way of seeing the digital tools we rely on—not as a wonder, or even as a villain, but rather as a series of choices that designers and technologists have made. Many of them seem small: what a button says, where a data set comes from. But each of those choices reinforces beliefs about the world, and the people in it.

It's up to us to demand that those choices be made differently—not because we want to see technology fail, but rather because we want it to succeed, on terms that work for all of us. After all, most of us don't hate tech. We love it. It's time we demand that it love us back.

Acknowledgments

Thank you to my editorial team: Alane Salierno Mason, for emailing me out of the blue and encouraging me to do this; and Ashley Patrick, for patiently answering my endless questions. Many thanks to my copy editor, Stephanie Hiebert, for bringing clarity and thoroughness to the manuscript (and for coining the delightful phrase "tenuous legitimacy at best," which is how I plan to describe myself from now on).

Endless gratitude to those who read early drafts: my love, William Bolton; and my friends Marie Connelly, Katel LeDû, Ethan Marcotte, and Mary Rohrdanz. I owe all of you wine, doughnuts, and hugs.

This book wouldn't have been possible without Eric Meyer. Collaborating with you on *Design for Real Life* changed the course of my career.

Thanks to those I spoke with during the writing process: Erin Abler, Jacky Alciné, Libby Bawcombe, Sally Jane Black, Anil Dash, Maggie Delano, Veronica Erb, Sorelle Friedler,

Aimee Gonzalez-Cameron, Lena Groeger, Sydette Harry, Dan Hon, Kate Kiefer Lee, Safiya Noble, Sally Rooney, Grace Sparapani, Kaya Thomas, Indi Young, and a whole host of wonderful people who shared their stories with me in confidence. I am also incredibly grateful to my friends Steve Fisher, Jason Santa Maria, and Matt Sutter for providing design help.

Thank you to the friends who gave feedback on all kinds of details, and who were there for me as I moaned and griped through this process—especially all the members of Camp Contentment, the Male Tears Club, Pizza Club, and the Ladies Anti-Fascist Friends Society. Cat-heart-eyes emoji for days.

Thank you to anyone I missed. I hope you forgive my terrible memory.

And, finally, thank you to everyone striving to make tech fairer, kinder, and more humane. I know we can do it.

Notes

Chapter 1: Welcome to the Machine

1. Andrew Perrin, "One-Fifth of Americans Report Going Online 'Almost Constantly,'" Pew Research Center, December 8, 2015, http://www.pewresearch.org/fact-tank/2015/12/08/one-fifth-of-amer icans-report-going-online-almost-constantly.
2. Oliver Wheaton, "Gym's Computer Assumed This Woman Was a Man Because She Is a Doctor," *Metro*, March 18, 2015, http://metro .co.uk/2015/03/18/gyms-computer-assumed-this-woman-was -a-man-because-she-is-a-doctor-5110391.
3. For an overview of the study's findings, see Pam Belluck, "Hey Siri, Can I Rely on You in a Crisis? Not Always, a Study Finds," March 14, 2016, *New York Times*, http://well.blogs.nytimes.com/2016/03/14/ hey-siri-can-i-rely-on-you-in-a-crisis-not-always-a-study-finds. The full study can be found in Adam S. Miner et al., "Smartphone-Based Conversational Agents and Responses to Questions about Mental Health, Interpersonal Violence, and Physical Health," *JAMA Internal Medicine* 176, no. 5 (2016): 619–25, http://jamanetwork .com/journals/jamainternalmedicine/article-abstract/2500043.
4. Anil Dash, "There Is No Technology Industry," *Humane Tech*, August 19, 2016, https://medium.com/humane-tech/there-is-no -technology-industry-44774dfb3ed7.

5. Safiya Noble, "Challenging the Algorithms of Oppression" (talk, Personal Democracy Forum, June 10, 2016), YouTube, June 15, 2016, https://www.youtube.com/watch?v=iRVZozEEWlE.

Chapter 2: Culture Misfit

1. Throughout the book, anecdotes that I relate without attribution were told to me in confidence—in person, by phone, or via email—and therefore remain anonymous. Some names have been changed to maintain that anonymity.
2. Amélie Lamont, "Not a Black Chair," Medium, March 14, 2016, https://medium.com/@amelielamont/not-a-black-chair-8a 8e7e2b9140#.gpk28w3fp.
3. Erica Joy, "The Other Side of Diversity," Medium, November 4, 2014, https://medium.com/this-is-hard/the-other-side-of-diversity-1bb 3de2f053e#.xn7th3cbt.
4. Megan Rose Dickey, "Apple's Tim Cook on Latest Diversity Numbers: There's 'a Lot More Work to be Done,'" *TechCrunch*, August 13, 2015, https://techcrunch.com/2015/08/13/apples-tim-cook-on-lat est-diversity-numbers-theres-a-lot-more-work-to-be-done.
5. Maxine Williams, "Facebook Diversity Update: Positive Hiring Trends Show Progress," Facebook Newsroom, July 14, 2016, http:// newsroom.fb.com/news/2016/07/facebook-diversity-update -positive-hiring-trends-show-progress.
6. Nancy Lee, "Focusing on Diversity," *The Keyword* (blog), June 30, 2016, https://www.blog.google/topics/diversity/focusing-on-div ersity30.
7. Apple, "Inclusion & Diversity," accessed October 15, 2016, http:// www.apple.com/diversity.
8. Google, "Diversity," accessed October 2016, https://www.google .com/diversity.
9. Airbnb, "Employee Diversity & Belonging: 2016 Assessment," October 25, 2016, http://blog.airbnb.com/employee-diversity-belong ing-2016-assesment.
10. Williams, "Facebook Diversity Update."
11. Kaya Thomas, "The Diverse Talent Pool Exists. Facebook Just Isn't Hiring Us," *Fusion*, July 15, 2016, http://fusion.net/story/325940/ the-diverse-talent-pool-exists.
12. Elizabeth Weise and Jessica Guynn, "Tech Jobs: Minorities Have Degrees, but Don't Get Hired," *USA Today*, October 12, 2014, http:// www.usatoday.com/story/tech/2014/10/12/silicon-valley-div

ersity-tech-hiring-computer-science-graduates-african-american-hispanic/14684211.

13. Thomas, "Diverse Talent Pool Exists."

14. Sarah Cooper, "Honest Diversity in Tech Report," *Cooper Review* (blog), accessed November 18, 2016, http://thecooperreview.com/diversity-in-tech-report.

15. Ellen Huet, "Facebook's Hiring Process Hinders Its Effort to Create a Diverse Workforce," *Bloomberg*, January 9, 2017, https://www.bloomberg.com/news/articles/2017-01-09/facebook-s-hiring-process-hinders-its-effort-to-create-a-diverse-workforce.

Chapter 3: Normal People

1. Maggie Delano, "I Tried Tracking My Period and It Was Even Worse Than I Could Have Imagined," Medium, February 23, 2015, https://medium.com/@maggied/i-tried-tracking-my-period-and-it-was-even-worse-than-i-could-have-imagined-bb46f869f45.

2. Glow, "About Glow," Wayback Machine, September 21, 2013, https://web.archive.org/web/20130921143302/https://www.glowing.com/about.

3. Kia Kokalitcheva, "Glow Brings in $17M in New Funding, Puts Big Data to Work for Women's Health," *VentureBeat*, October 2, 2014, http://venturebeat.com/2014/10/02/glow-brings-in-17m-in-new-funding-as-puts-big-data-to-task-with-fertility-challenges.

4. Glow, "About Glow," Wayback Machine, March 27, 2014, https://web.archive.org/web/20140327011628/https://glowing.com/about.

5. Erin Abler, Twitter post, January 31, 2017 (6:12 p.m.), https://twitter.com/erinabler/status/826614200114016256.

6. Michael M. Grynbaum, "New York's Cabbies Like Credit Cards? Go Figure," *New York Times*, November 7, 2009, http://www.nytimes.com/2009/11/08/nyregion/08taxi.html.

7. Lena Groeger, "Set It and Forget It: How Default Settings Rule the World," *ProPublica*, July 27, 2016, https://www.propublica.org/article/set-it-and-forget-it-how-default-settings-rule-the-world.

8. Madeline Messer, "I'm a 12-Year-Old Girl. Why Don't the Characters in My Apps Look Like Me?" *Washington Post*, March 4, 2015, https://www.washingtonpost.com/posteverything/wp/2015/03/04/im-a-12-year-old-girl-why-dont-the-characters-in-my-apps-look-like-me.

9. Adrienne LaFrance, "Why Do So Many Digital Assistants Have Feminine Names?" *Atlantic*, March 30, 2016, http://www.the

atlantic.com/technology/archive/2016/03/why-do-so-many
-digital-assistants-have-feminine-names/475884.

10. For a whole ton of examples, see Neha Prakash, "Snapchat Faces an Outcry against 'Whitewashing' Filters," *Mashable*, May 16, 2016, http://mashable.com/2016/05/16/snapchat-whitewashing/#pLqU ZA7KJuqs.

11. Jessica Nordell, "Stop Giving Digital Assistants Female Voices," *New Republic*, June 23, 2016, https://newrepublic.com/article/ 134560/stop-giving-digital-assistants-female-voices.

12. Todd Rose, *The End of Average: How to Succeed in a World That Values Sameness* (New York: HarperCollins, 2016).

13. Libby Bawcombe, "Designing New Products with Empathy: 50 Stress Cases to Consider," Design at NPR, August 16, 2016, https:// npr.design/designing-news-products-with-empathy-50-stress- cases-to-consider-61f068a939eb. © 2016 National Public Radio, Inc. Used with the permission of NPR. Any unauthorized duplica- tion is strictly prohibited.

14. Ibid.

15. Libby Bawcombe, email to the author, December 10, 2016.

16. Indi Young, "Describing Personas," Medium, March 15, 2016, https: //medium.com/@indiyoung/describing-personas-af992e3fc527#. vw2pgmvm5.

17. Shonda Rhimes, "You Are Not Alone," Medium, March 16, 2015, https://medium.com/thelist/you-are-not-alone-69c1a10515ab# .r9gaxhcei.

Chapter 4: Select One

1. Shane Creepingbear, Twitter post, October 13, 2014 (7:43 p.m.), https://twitter.com/Creepingbear/status/521853766803673088.

2. Shane Creepingbear, "The Removal of American Indians from Face- book," Last Real Indians, accessed November 3, 2016, http:// lastrealindians.com/the-removal-of-american-indians-from-face book-by-shane-creepingbear.

3. Chris Cox, Facebook post, October 1, 2014, https://www.facebook .com/chris.cox/posts/10101301777354543.

4. Chris Matyszczyk, "Batman's Fight to Get on Facebook," *CNET*, March 8, 2009, https://www.cnet.com/news/batmans-fight-to -get-on-facebook.

5. Justin Osofsky and Todd Gage, "Community Support FYI: Improv- ing the Names Process on Facebook," Facebook Newsroom, Decem-

ber 15, 2015, http://newsroom.fb.com/news/2015/12/community
-support-fyi-improving-the-names-process-on-facebook.

6. Jens Manuel Krogstad and D'Vera Cohn, "U.S. Census Looking at
   Big Changes in How It Asks about Race and Ethnicity," Pew Research
   Center, March 14, 2014, http://www.pewresearch.org/fact-tank
   /2014/03/14/u-s-census-looking-at-big-changes-in-how-it-asks-
   about-race-and-ethnicity.

7. Pew Research Center, "Multiracial in America: Proud, Diverse and
   Growing in Numbers," June 11, 2015, http://www.pewsocialtrends
   .org/2015/06/11/multiracial-in-america.

8. Jamelle Bouie, "What Pundits Keep Getting Wrong about Donald
   Trump and the Working Class," *Slate*, May 5, 2016, http://www.slate
   .com/articles/news_and_politics/politics/2016/05/what_pundits_
   keep_getting_wrong_about_donald_trump_and_the_working_
   class.html.

9. Renee Stepler and Anna Brown, "Statistical Portrait of Hispanics in
   the United States," Pew Research Center, April 19, 2016, http://www
   .pewhispanic.org/2016/04/19/statistical-portrait-of-hispanics
   -in-the-united-states.

10. Jeffrey S. Passel and D'Vera Cohn, "U.S. Population Projections:
    2005–2050," Pew Research Center, February 11, 2008, http://www
    .pewhispanic.org/2008/02/11/us-population-projections
    -2005-2050.

11. Andrew R. Flores et al., "How Many Adults Identify as Transgender
    in the United States?" Williams Institute, UCLA School of Law, June
    2016, http://williamsinstitute.law.ucla.edu/wp-content/uploads/
    How-Many-Adults-Identify-as-Transgender-in-the-United-States
    .pdf.

12. Jan Hoffman, "Estimate of U.S. Transgender Population Doubles to
    1.4 Million Adults," *New York Times*, July 1, 2016, http://www
    .nytimes.com/2016/07/01/health/transgender-population.html.

13. Alexandra Buxton, "Mistress, Miss, Mrs or Ms: Untangling the
    Shifting History of Women's Titles," *New Statesman*, September 12,
    2014, http://www.newstatesman.com/cultural-capital/2014/09/
    mistress-miss-mrs-or-ms-untangling-shifting-history-women-s-
    titles.

14. GOV.UK Service Manual, "Names," accessed February 13, 2017,
    https://www.gov.uk/service-manual/design/names.

15. Caroline O'Donovan, "Nextdoor Rolls Out Product Fix It Hopes
    Will Stem Racial Profiling," *BuzzFeed*, August 24, 2016, https://

www.buzzfeed.com/carolineodonovan/nextdoor-rolls-out-product
-fix-it-hopes-will-stem-racial-pro.

16. See the post about the updates in "Our Commitment to End Racial
Profiling on Nextdoor," *Nextdoor Blog*, January 27, 2016, https://
blog.nextdoor.com/2016/01/27/our-commitment-to-end-racial
-profiling-on-nextdoor.

17. Nirav Tolia, "Reducing Racial Profiling on Nextdoor," *Nextdoor
Blog*, August 24, 2016, https://blog.nextdoor.com/2016/08/24/
reducing-racial-profiling-on-nextdoor.

18. Margaret Rhodes, "Nextdoor Breaks a Sacred Design Rule to End
Racial Profiling," *Wired*, August 31, 2016, https://www.wired
.com/2016/08/nextdoor-breaks-sacred-design-rule-end-ra
cial-profiling.

19. Aimee Gonzalez-Cameron, phone interview with the author,
November 14, 2016.

20. Emily Horseman, "The Argument for Free-Form Input," *Model
View Culture*, November 23, 2015, https://modelviewculture.com/
pieces/the-argument-for-free-form-input.

21. Rhodes, "Nextdoor Breaks a Sacred Design Rule."

Chapter 5: Delighted to Death

1. Dan Hon, Twitter post, October 10, 2016 (10:38 p.m.), https://twitter
.com/hondanhon/status/785668423099428864.

2. Dan Hon, Twitter post, October 10, 2016 (10:03 p.m.), https://twitter
.com/hondanhon/status/785662188178411521.

3. Timehop, [homepage], April 13, 2017, http://www.timehop.com.

4. Mike Babb, Twitter post, June 3, 2016 (4:08 a.m.), https://twitter
.com/mikegbabb/status/738688748494327811.

5. Ibid.

6. All the videos I reference are embedded in this article: Adam Boult,
"Facebook Makes Oddly Cheerful Video from Man's Horrific Car
Crash Photos," *Telegraph*, September 13, 2016, http://www.telegraph
.co.uk/news/2016/09/13/facebook-makes-oddly-cheerful-video
-from-mans-horrific-car-crash.

7. Sally Rooney, email to the author, January 11, 2017.

8. Kiefer Lee, phone interview with the author, June 24, 2015.

9. Ibid.

10. Jesse Charger, "Negging Women—10 Awesome Negs That Work,"
Seduction Science, accessed December 2016, http://www.seduction
science.com/2010/negging-women.

11. Arien Mack and Irvin Rock, *Inattentional Blindness* (Cambridge, MA: MIT Press, 1998).

12. Christopher Chabris and Daniel Simons, *The Invisible Gorilla: How Our Intuitions Deceive Us* (New York: Harmony, 2011). For the original video: Daniel Simons, "Selective Attention Test," YouTube, March 10, 2010, https://www.youtube.com/watch?v=vJG698U2Mvo.

13. Alix Spiegel, "Why Even Radiologists Can Miss a Gorilla Hiding in Plain Sight," *Shots*, NPR, February 11, 2013, http://www.npr.org/sections/health-shots/2013/02/11/171409656/why-even-radiologists-can-miss-a-gorilla-hiding-in-plain-sight.

14. Cory Weinberg and Amir Efrati, "Inside Facebook's Campaign to Convince You It Cares," *The Information*, January 14, 2016, https://www.theinformation.com/inside-facebooks-campaign-to-convince-you-it-cares.

15. Julianne Tveten, "The Rise of Confirmshaming: When Websites Insult You for Not Opting In," *Motherboard*, June 7, 2016, http://motherboard.vice.com/read/confirmshaming.

16. Tag Savage, Twitter post, September 4, 2016 (11:30 a.m.), https://twitter.com/tagsavage/status/772504445406048257.

Chapter 6: Tracked, Tagged, and Targeted

1. Julia Angwin, Terry Parris Jr., and Surya Mattu, "Facebook Doesn't Tell Users Everything It Really Knows about Them," *ProPublica*, December 27, 2016, https://www.propublica.org/article/facebook-doesnt-tell-users-everything-it-really-knows-about-them.

2. Natasha Singer, "Mapping, and Sharing, the Consumer Genome," *New York Times*, June 16, 2012, http://www.nytimes.com/2012/06/17/technology/acxiom-the-quiet-giant-of-consumer-database-marketing.html.

3. Acxiom Corporation, "Personicx Online Guide: 06 Casual Comfort," 2014.

4. If you're not sure how important this is, read security expert Bruce Schneier's *Data and Goliath: The Hidden Battles to Collect Your Data and Control Your World* (New York: W. W. Norton, 2016). Twenty bucks says you'll want to throw your phone in a river and move to a cabin off the grid by the time you're done.

5. Andrew J. Hawkins, "Uber Wants to Track Your Location Even When You're Not Using the App," *Verge*, November 30, 2016, http://www.theverge.com/2016/11/30/13763714/uber-location-data-tracking-app-privacy-ios-android.

6. Jon Russell, "Uber's Moral Compass Needs Recalibration," *Tech-Crunch*, November 19, 2014, https://techcrunch.com/2014/11/19/uber-off.

7. Kai Ryssdal, "Uber's Data Makes a Creepy Point about the Company," *Marketplace*, Minnesota Public Radio, November 18, 2014, http://www.marketplace.org/2014/11/18/business/final-note/ubers-data-makes-creepy-point-about-company.

8. Tim Jones, "Facebook's 'Evil Interfaces,'" *Deeplinks* (blog), Electronic Frontier Foundation, April 29, 2010, https://www.eff.org/deeplinks/2010/04/facebooks-evil-interfaces.

9. "Facebook Asks More than 350 Million Users around the World to Personalize Their Privacy," Facebook Newsroom, December 9, 2009, https://newsroom.fb.com/news/2009/12/facebook-asks-more-than-350-million-users-around-the-world-to-personalize-their-privacy.

10. Cecilia Kang, "Google Tracks Consumers' Online Activities across Products, and Users Can't Opt Out," *Washington Post*, January 24, 2012, https://www.washingtonpost.com/business/technology/google-tracks-consumers-across-products-users-cant-opt-out/2012/01/24/gIQArgJHOQ_story.html.

11. Sarah Kessler, "Google Thinks I'm a Middle-Aged Man. What about You?" *Mashable*, January 25, 2012, http://mashable.com/2012/01/25/google-cookies/#MhtR2DYc3kqg.

12. Cathy O'Neil, *Weapons of Math Destruction: How Big Data Increases Inequality and Threatens Democracy* (New York: Crown, 2016).

13. Julia Angwin and Terry Parris Jr., "Facebook Lets Advertisers Exclude Users by Race," *ProPublica*, October 28, 2016, https://www.propublica.org/article/facebook-lets-advertisers-exclude-users-by-race.

14. Safiya Noble, phone interview with the author, January 9, 2017.

15. Jesse Barron, "The Babysitters Club," *Real Life*, July 27, 2016, http://reallifemag.com/the-babysitters-club.

16. Ibid.

17. Ibid.

18. See Pew Research Center, "Mobile Fact Sheet," accessed January 12, 2017, http://www.pewinternet.org/fact-sheet/mobile.

19. O'Neil, *Weapons of Math Destruction*, conclusion.

Chapter 7: Algorithmic Inequity

1. Both men's offenses are outlined in Julia Angwin et al., "What Algo-

rithmic Injustice Looks Like in Real Life," *Pacific Standard*, June 2, 2016, https://psmag.com/what-algorithmic-injustice-looks-like-in -real-life-c58d409aa4dc#.5vh2au6z2.

2. Julia Angwin et al., "Machine Bias," *ProPublica*, May 23, 2016, https://www.propublica.org/article/machine-bias-risk-assess ments-in-criminal-sentencing.

3. According to NAACP, "Criminal Justice Fact Sheet," accessed January 30, 2017, http://www.naacp.org/criminal-justice-fact-sheet.

4. Cathy O'Neil, *Weapons of Math Destruction: How Big Data Increases Inequality and Threatens Democracy* (New York: Crown, 2016), conclusion.

5. Northpointe, "COMPAS Risk & Need Assessment System: Selected Questions Posed by Inquiring Agencies," 2012, http://www .northpointeinc.com/files/downloads/FAQ_Document.pdf.

6. Sam Corbett-Davies et al., "A Computer Program Used for Bail and Sentencing Decisions Was Labeled Biased against Blacks. It's Actually Not That Clear," *Washington Post*, October 17, 2016, https:// www.washingtonpost.com/news/monkey-cage/wp/2016/10/17/ can-an-algorithm-be-racist-our-analysis-is-more-cautious-than-propublicas.

7. Julia Angwin and Jeff Larson, "Bias in Criminal Risk Scores Is Mathematically Inevitable, Researchers Say," *ProPublica*, December 30, 2016, https://www.propublica.org/article/bias-in-criminal -risk-scores-is-mathematically-inevitable-researchers-say.

8. Sorelle Friedler, phone interview with the author, January 30, 2017.

9. "Why Google 'Thought' This Black Woman Was a Gorilla," *Note to Self*, WNYC, September 28, 2015, http://www.wnyc.org/story/ deep-problem-deep-learning.

10. Jacky Alciné, email to the author, January 27, 2017.

11. Google Photos, [product tour screens], accessed January 28, 2017, https://photos.google.com.

12. For a walk through the basics, see the free online book by Michael Nielsen: *Neural Networks and Deep Learning* (Determination Press, 2015), http://neuralnetworksanddeeplearning.com.

13. Daniela Hernandez, "The New Google Photos App Is Disturbingly Good at Data-Mining Your Photos," *Fusion*, June 4, 2015, http:// fusion.net/story/142326/the-new-google-photos-app-is-dis turbingly-good-at-data-mining-your-photos.

14. Fei-Fei Li tells the story of bringing this sort of neural network to life in her 2015 TED talk: "How We're Teaching Computers to Under-

stand Pictures," March 2015, https://www.ted.com/talks/fei_fei_li_how_we_re_teaching_computers_to_understand_pictures/transcript.

15. "Google Apologises for Photos App's Racist Blunder," *BBC News*, July 1, 2015, http://www.bbc.com/news/technology-33347866.

16. Yonatan Zunger, Twitter post, June 29, 2015 (11:19 a.m.), https://twitter.com/yonatanzunger/status/615585375487045632.

17. Mandelit del Barco, "How Kodak's Shirley Cards Set Photography's Skin-Tone Standard," *Color Decoded: Stories That Span the Spectrum*, NPR, November 13, 2014, http://www.npr.org/2014/11/13/363517842/for-decades-kodak-s-shirley-cards-set-photography-s-skin-tone-standard.

18. Lorna Roth, "Looking at Shirley, the Ultimate Norm: Colour Balance, Image Technologies, and Cognitive Equity," *Canadian Journal of Communication* 34, no. 1 (2009): 111–36, http://www.cjc-online.ca/index.php/journal/article/view/2196/3069.

19. Ibid.

20. Yonatan Zunger, Twitter posts: June 29, 2015 (11:23 a.m.), https://twitter.com/yonatanzunger/status/615586442413146112; and June 29, 2015 (11:24 a.m.), https://twitter.com/yonatanzunger/status/615586630842236928.

21. Andrew Griffin, "Flickr's Auto-tagging Feature Goes Awry, Accidentally Tags Black People as Apes," *Independent*, May 20, 2015, http://www.independent.co.uk/life-style/gadgets-and-tech/news/flickr-s-auto-tagging-feature-goes-awry-accidentally-tags-black-people-as-apes-10264144.html.

22. Odelia Lee, "Camera Misses the Mark on Racial Sensitivity," *Gizmodo*, May 15, 2009, http://gizmodo.com/5256650/camera-misses-the-mark-on-racial-sensitivity.

23. See "HP Computers Are Racist," YouTube, December 10, 2009, https://www.youtube.com/watch?v=t4DT3tQqgRM.

24. Friedler, phone interview, January 30, 2017.

25. Rose Eveleth, "The Inherent Bias of Facial Recognition," *Motherboard*, March 21, 2016, http://motherboard.vice.com/read/the-inherent-bias-of-facial-recognition.

26. Tolga Bolukbasi et al., "Man Is to Computer Programmer as Woman Is to Homemaker? Debiasing Word Embeddings," July 21, 2016, https://arxiv.org/pdf/1607.06520v1.pdf.

27. Rob May, "Introducing CV2Vec: A Neural Model for Candidate Similarity," Medium, May 12, 2016, https://medium.com/talla-inc/

introducing-cv2vec-a-neural-model-for-candidate-similarity-e215b1b12472#.bkh1bb45w.

28. Rob May, "Artificial Intelligence in HR," *HR Examiner*, March 2, 2017, http://www.hrexaminer.com/artificial-intelligence-in-hr.
29. Bolukbasi et al., "Man Is to Computer Programmer," 3.
30. David A. Graham, "The White-Supremacist Group That Inspired a Racist Manifesto," *Atlantic*, June 22, 2015, http://www.theatlantic.com/politics/archive/2015/06/council-of-conservative-citizens-dylann-roof/396467.
31. From Dylann Roof's manifesto, originally published on his site, http://www.lastrhodesian.com. A cached version was saved June 20, 2015, after his arrest, at http://archive.is/KeAK3.
32. Miriam E. Sweeney, "Not Just a Pretty (Inter)Face: A Critical Analysis of Microsoft's 'Ms. Dewey,'" (PhD diss., University of Illinois at Urbana-Champaign, 2013), https://www.ideals.illinois.edu/bitstream/handle/2142/46617/Miriam_Sweeney.pdf.
33. Kristen Purcell, Joanna Brenner, and Lee Rainie, "Search Engine Use 2012," Pew Research Center, http://www.pewinternet.org/2012/03/09/search-engine-use-2012.
34. Edelman, "2017 Edelman Trust Barometer: Global Annual Study," January 15, 2017, http://www.edelman.com/trust2017.
35. Stephen Levy, *In the Plex: How Google Thinks, Works, and Shapes Our Lives* (New York: Simon & Schuster, 2011), 206–7.\
36. Northpointe, "COMPAS Risk & Need Assessment System: Selected Questions Posed by Inquiring Agencies," January 14, 2010, http://www.northpointeinc.com/files/technical_documents/Selected_Compas_Questions_Posed_by_Inquiring_Agencies.pdf.
37. Eveleth, "Inherent Bias of Facial Recognition."
38. Friedler, phone interview, January 30, 2017.
39. Ibid.

Chapter 8: Built to Break

1. Lindy West, "Twitter Doesn't Think These Rape and Death Threats Are Harassment," *Daily Dot*, December 23, 2014, http://www.dailydot.com/via/twitter-harassment-rape-death-threat-report.
2. Natasha Tiku and Casey Newton, "Twitter CEO: 'We Suck at Dealing with Abuse,'" *Verge*, February 4, 2015, http://www.theverge.com/2015/2/4/7982099/twitter-ceo-sent-memo-taking-personal-responsibility-for-the.
3. Maeve Duggan, "Online Harassment," Pew Research Center, Octo-

ber 22, 2014, http://www.pewinternet.org/2014/10/22/online
-harassment.

4. Lindy West, "I've Left Twitter. It Is Unusable for Anyone but Trolls,
Robots and Dictators," *Guardian*, January 3, 2017, https://www.
theguardian.com/commentisfree/2017/jan/03/ive-left-twitter
-unusable-anyone-but-trolls-robots-dictators-lindy-west.

5. If you truly can't help yourself, see these two *Breitbart* articles by
Yiannopoulos: "Teenage Boys with Tits: Here's My Problem with
Ghostbusters," July 18, 2016, http://www.breitbart.com/tech/
2016/07/18/milo-reviews-ghostbusters; and "Here's Why the Left Is
So Desperate to Defend the New Feminist Ghostbusters," May 5,
2016, http://www.breitbart.com/milo/2016/05/05/heres-left-des
perate-defend-new-feminist-ghostbusters.

6. Leslie Jones, Twitter posts: July 18, 2016 (9:44 p.m.), https://twitter
.com/Lesdoggg/status/755261962674696192; and July 18, 2016
(10:20 p.m.), https://twitter.com/Lesdoggg/status/75527100452
0349698.

7. Charlie Warzel, "Twitter Permanently Suspends Conservative
Writer Milo Yiannopoulos," *BuzzFeed*, July 19, 2016, https://www.
buzzfeed.com/charliewarzel/twitter-just-permanently-suspended
-conservative-writer-milo.

8. Kerry Flynn, "Twitter's Biggest Anti-troll Effort to Date Is Finally
Here," *Mashable*, November 15, 2016, http://mashable.com/
2016/11/15/twitter-abuse-updates/#15Fs6Om838qP.

9. Ed Ho, "An Update on Safety," *Official Twitter Blog*, February 7, 2017,
https://blog.twitter.com/2017/an-update-on-safety.

10. Laurie Penny, "I'm with the Banned," *Welcome to the Scream Room*,
July 21, 2016, https://medium.com/welcome-to-the-scream-room/
im-with-the-banned-8d1b6e0b2932#.h3k5r59gr.

11. Diana Tourjee, "Trans Student Harassed by Milo Yiannopoulos
Speaks Out," *Broadly*, January 3, 2017, https://broadly.vice.com/
en_us/article/trans-student-harassed-by-milo-yiannopoulos
-speaks-out.

12. Maya Oppenheim, "UC Berkeley Protests: Milo Yiannopoulos
Planned to 'Publicy [*sic*] Name Undocumented Students' in Cancelled
Talk," *Independent*, February 3, 2017, http://www.independent.co.uk
/news/world/americas/uc-berkely-protests-milo-yiannopoulos
-publicly-name-undocumented-students-cancelled-talk-illegals
-a7561321.html.

13. Donald J. Trump, Twitter post, February 2, 2017 (3:13 a.m.), https://
twitter.com/realdonaldtrump/status/827112633224544256.

14. David Sarno, "Twitter Creator Jack Dorsey Illuminates the Site's Founding Document. Part I," *Technology* (blog), *Los Angeles Times*, February 18, 2009, http://latimesblogs.latimes.com/technology/2009/02/twitter-creator.html.

15. Jack Dorsey, "Twittr Sketch," Flickr, March 24, 2006, https://www.flickr.com/photos/jackdorsey/182613360.

16. Nick Douglas, "Twitter Blows Up at SXSW Conference," *Gawker* (blog), March 12, 2007, http://gawker.com/243634/twitter-blows-up-at-sxsw-conference.

17. Aaron Smith, "Twitter Update 2011," Pew Research Center, June 1, 2011, http://www.pewinternet.org/2011/06/01/twitter-update-2011.

18. Twitter, [homepage], Wayback Machine, February 2, 2007, https://web.archive.org/web/20070202022702/www.twitter.com.

19. Lucy Battersby, "Twitter Criticised for Failing to Respond to Caroline Criado-Perez Rape Threats," *Age*, July 29, 2013, http://www.theage.com.au/digital-life/digital-life-news/twitter-criticised-for-failing-to-respond-to-caroline-criadoperez-rape-threats-20130729-2qu8d.html.

20. Josh Halliday, "Twitter's Tony Wang: 'We Are the Free Speech Wing of the Free Speech Party,'" *Guardian*, March 22, 2012, https://www.theguardian.com/media/2012/mar/22/twitter-tony-wang-free-speech.

21. A good overview of Gamergate for the uninitiated can be found in Caitlin Dewey, "The Only Guide to Gamergate You Will Ever Need to Read," *Washington Post*, October 14, 2014, https://www.washingtonpost.com/news/the-intersect/wp/2014/10/14/the-only-guide-to-gamergate-you-will-ever-need-to-read.

22. Charlie Warzel, "A Honeypot for Assholes: Inside Twitter's 10-Year Failure to Stop Harassment," *BuzzFeed*, August 11, 2016, https://www.buzzfeed.com/charliewarzel/a-honeypot-for-assholes-inside-twitters-10-year-failure-to-s.

23. Ibid.

24. For just a few of the many, many articles, see Robinson Meyer, "The Decay of Twitter," *Atlantic*, November 2, 2015, https://www.theatlantic.com/technology/archive/2015/11/conversation-smoosh-twitter-decay/412867; Casey Newton and Nilay Patel, "Is Twitter Doomed?" *Verge*, January 26, 2016, www.theverge.com/2016/1/26/10833024/is-twitter-doomed; and Hayley Tsukayama, "The Death of Twitter as We Know It," *Washington Post*, February 11, 2016, https://www.washingtonpost.com/news/the-switch/wp/2016/02/11/the-death-of-twitter-as-we-know-it.

25. Vindu Goel, "Dismal Twitter Forecast and Flat User Growth Send Its Stock Lower," *New York Times,* October 27, 2015, https://www .nytimes.com/2015/10/28/technology/twitter-q3-earnings.html.

26. Alex Sherman, Christopher Palmeri, and Sarah Frier, "Disney Dropped Twitter Pursuit Partly over Image," *Bloomberg,* October 17, 2016, https://www.bloomberg.com/news/articles/2016-10-17/ disney-said-to-have-dropped-twitter-pursuit-partly-over-image.

27. Eugene Kim, "Twitter Trolls Were Part of the Reason Why Salesforce Walked Away from a Deal," *Business Insider,* October 17, 2016, http://www.businessinsider.com/twitter-trolls-caused-salesforce -to-walk-away-from-deal-2016-10.

28. Twitter Safety, Twitter post, February 13, 2017 (1:02 p.m.), https:// twitter.com/TwitterSafety/status/831247282544599040.

29. Ariel Bogle, "Twitter Launches, and Then Kills, an Anti-abuse Effort within Hours," *Mashable,* February 13, 2017, http://mashable. com/2017/02/13/twitter-list-notifications-abuse/#Fd1zC9Wl3mqd.

30. Alexa, "Reddit.com Traffic Statistics," accessed February 17, 2017, http://www.alexa.com/siteinfo/reddit.com.

31. Sarah Jeong, "Après moi, le déluge: What Went Wrong on Reddit," *Forbes,* July 15, 2015, http://www.forbes.com/sites/sarahjeong /2015/07/15/apres-moi-le-deluge-what-went-wrong-on-reddit/ #49c38d1670fe.

32. Reddit, "Removing Harassing Subreddits," Reddit post: r/announce-ments, June 10, 2015, https://www.reddit.com/r/announcements/ comments/39bpam/removing_harassing_subreddits.

33. Jeong, "Après moi, le déluge."

34. David Spinks, "Distributed Control: How Reddit Is Taking the Management Out of Community Management," CMX, June 9, 2014, http://cmxhub.com/erik-martin-reddit-community-interview.

35. Seth Fiegerman, "Aliens in the Valley: The Complete History of Reddit, the Internet's Front Page," *Mashable,* December 13, 2014, http:// mashable.com/2014/12/03/history-of-reddit.

36. Aaron Sankin, "As Racist, Sexist Trolls Infest Reddit, Admins Do Nothing," *Daily Dot,* August 27, 2014, http://www.dailydot.com/irl/ reddit-rape-racist-comment-trolls-problem.

37. pro_creator (moderator), "We Have a Racist User Problem and Reddit Won't Take Action," Reddit post: r/blackladies, August 25, 2014, https://www.reddit.com/r/blackladies/comments/2ejg1b/we_have _a_racist_user_problem_and_reddit_wont.

38. Jeong, "Après moi, le déluge."

39. Sarah Jeong, *The Internet of Garbage*, Forbes Signature Series (Jersey City, NJ: Forbes Media, 2015).
40. Nick Statt, "Reddit Bans Two Prominent Alt-Right Subreddits," *Verge*, February 1, 2017, http://www.theverge.com/2017/2/1/1447 8948/reddit-alt-right-ban-altright-alternative-right-subreddits -doxing.
41. Alexis Ohanian, "An Open Letter to the Reddit Community," Reddit post: r/blog, January 30, 2017, https://www.reddit.com/r/blog/ comments/5r43td/an_open_letter_to_the_reddit_community.
42. Craig Silverman, "This Analysis Shows How Viral Fake Election News Stories Outperformed Real News on Facebook," *BuzzFeed*, November 16, 2016, https://www.buzzfeed.com/craigsilverman/ viral-fake-election-news-outperformed-real-news-on-facebook.
43. Michael Nuñez, "Former Facebook Workers: We Routinely Suppressed Conservative News," *Gizmodo*, May 9, 2016, http://gizmodo. com/former-facebook-workers-we-routinely-suppressed-conser -1775461006.
44. Senator John Thune to Mark Zuckerberg, May 10, 2016, http://www. commerce.senate.gov/public/_cache/files/fe5b7b75-8d53-44c3- 8a20-6b2c12b0970d/C5CF587E2778E073A80A79E2A6F73705. fb-letter.pdf.
45. Joon Ian Wong, Dave Gershgorn, and Mike Murphy, "Facebook Is Trying to Get Rid of Bias in Trending News by Getting Rid of Humans," *Quartz*, August 26, 2016, https://qz.com/768122/face book-fires-human-editors-moves-to-algorithm-for-trending-topics.
46. Abby Ohlheiser, "Three Days after Removing Human Editors, Facebook Is Already Trending Fake News," *Washington Post*, August 29, 2016, https://www.washingtonpost.com/news/the-intersect/wp/ 2016/08/29/a-fake-headline-about-megyn-kelly-was-trending-on- facebook.
47. Michael Nuñez, "Want to Know What Facebook Really Thinks of Journalists? Here's What Happened When It Hired Some," *Gizmodo*, May 3, 2016, http://gizmodo.com/want-to-know-what-face book-really-thinks-of-journalists-1773916117.
48. Will Oremus, "Trending Bad: How Facebook's Foray into Automated News Went from Messy to Disastrous," *Slate*, August 30, 2016, http://www.slate.com/articles/technology/future_tense/2016/08/ how_facebook_s_trending_news_feature_went_from_messy_to_ disastrous.html.
49. Victor Luckerson, "Here's Why Facebook Won't Put Your News Feed

in Chronological Order," *Time*, July 9, 2015, http://time.com/ 3951337/facebook-chronological-order.

50. Josh Constine, "Facebook's S-1 Letter from Zuckerberg Urges Understanding before Investment," *TechCrunch*, February 1, 2012, https://techcrunch.com/2012/02/01/facebook-ipo-letter.

51. Mark Zuckerberg, "Building Global Community," Facebook post, February 16, 2017, https://www.facebook.com/notes/mark-zucker berg/building-global-community/10154544292806634.

52. "When FOMO Meets JOMO," *Note to Self*, WNYC, January 20, 2016, http://www.wnyc.org/story/fomo-jomo.

Chapter 9: Meritocracy Now, Meritocracy Forever

1. From Brian S. Hall's now-deleted article in *Forbes*, "There Is No Diversity Crisis in Tech," which he reposted at Medium.com on October 7, 2015: https://medium.com/@brianshall/the-article-on- diversity-in-tech-that-forbes-took-down-15cfd28d5639# .sp3ogqmuw.

2. Michael Young, "Down with Meritocracy," *Guardian*, June 28, 2001, https://www.theguardian.com/politics/2001/jun/29/comment.

3. Sarah McBride, "Insight: In Silicon Valley Start-up World, Pedigree Counts," *Reuters*, September 12, 2013, http://www.reuters.com/ article/us-usa-startup-connections-insight-idUSBRE98 B15U20130912.

4. Vivek Wadhwa, "Silicon Valley: You and Some of Your VC's Have a Gender Problem," *TechCrunch*, February 7, 2010, https://techcrunch .com/2010/02/07/silicon-valley-you%E2%80%99ve-got -a-gender-problem-and-some-of-your-vc%E2%80%99s-still-live- in-the-past.

5. Claire Burke and Kate Dwyer, "2016 Review of Female Founders Raising Institutional Capital," Female Founders Fund, February 1, 2017, http://femalefoundersfund.com/2016-review-of-female-foun ders-raising-institutional-capital/#sthash.Snz0RmSe.dpbs.

6. Kim-Mai Cutler, "Sexism in the Venture Business? Sequoia's Greg McAdoo Says VC Industry Is a 'Meritocracy,'" *TechCrunch*, May 23, 2012, https://techcrunch.com/2012/05/23/no-sexism-here-sequoi as-greg-mcadoo-says-venture-business-is-a-meritocracy.

7. Jodo Kantor, "A Brand New World in Which Men Ruled," *New York Times*, December 23, 2014, https://www.nytimes.com/interactive/ 2014/12/23/us/gender-gaps-stanford-94.html.

8. Lauren Orsini, "Why GitHub's CEO Ditched Its Divisive 'Meritoc-

racy' Rug," *ReadWrite*, January 24, 2014, http://readwrite.com/2014/01/24/github-meritocracy-rug.

9. Adrienne LaFrance, "Is Silicon Valley a Meritocracy?" *Atlantic*, October 13, 2016, https://www.theatlantic.com/technology/archive/2016/10/is-silicon-valley-a-meritocracy/503948.

10. Susan J. Fowler, "Reflecting on One Very, Very Strange Year at Uber," *Susan J. Fowler* (blog), February 19, 2017, https://www.susanjfowler.com/blog/2017/2/19/reflecting-on-one-very-strange-year-at-uber.

11. Everett Rosenfeld, "Uber CEO Orders 'Urgent Investigation' after Allegation of Harassment, Gender Bias at Company," CNBC, February 19, 2017, http://www.cnbc.com/2017/02/19/uber-ceo-travis-kalanick-says-orders-urgent-investigation-after-allegation-of-harassment-gender-bias-at-company.html.

12. Steven Overly, "Uber Hires Eric Holder to Investigate Sexual Harassment Claims," *Washington Post*, February 21, 2017, https://www.washingtonpost.com/news/innovations/wp/2017/02/21/uber-hires-eric-holder-to-investigate-sexual-harassment-claims.

13. Kara Swisher, "Uber's SVP of Engineering Is Out After He Did Not Disclose He Left Google in a Dispute over a Sexual Harassment Allegation," *Recode*, February 27, 2017, http://www.recode.net/2017/2/27/14745360/amit-singhal-google-uber.

14. Eric Newcomer and Olivia Zaleski, "When Their Shifts End, Uber Drivers Set Up Camp in Parking Lots across the U.S.," *Bloomberg*, January 23, 2017, https://www.bloomberg.com/news/articles/2017-01-23/when-their-shifts-end-uber-drivers-set-up-camp-in-parking-lots-across-the-u-s.

15. Johana Bhuiyan, "For Some People Looking to Dump Uber, the #deleteUber Campaign Simply Sealed the Deal," *Recode*, January 30, 2017, https://www.recode.net/2017/1/30/14445122/delete-uber-trump-protest-immigration-ban.

16. Mike Isaac, "Uber C.E.O. to Leave Trump Advisory Council after Criticism," *New York Times*, February 2, 2017, https://www.nytimes.com/2017/02/02/technology/uber-ceo-travis-kalanick-trump-advisory-council.html.

17. Eric Newcomer, "In Video, Uber CEO Argues with Driver over Falling Fares," *Bloomberg*, February 28, 2017, https://www.bloomberg.com/news/articles/2017-02-28/in-video-uber-ceo-argues-with-driver-over-falling-fares.

18. Travis Kalanick, "A Profound Apology," *Uber Newsroom* (blog), February 28, 2017, https://newsroom.uber.com/a-profound-apology.

19. Mickey Rapkin, "Uber Cab Confessions," *GQ*, February 27, 2014, http://www.gq.com/story/uber-cab-confessions.

20. Nitasha Tiku, "Uber CEO on Driver 'Assault': It's Not Real and We're Not Responsible," *Valleywag*, September 16, 2013, http://valleywag.gawker.com/uber-ceo-on-driver-assault-its-not-real-and-were-n-1323533057.

21. Alison Griswold, "Uber Is Designed So That for One Employee to Get Ahead, Another Must Fail," *Quartz*, February 27, 2017, https://qz.com/918582/uber-is-designed-so-that-for-one-employee-to-succeed-another-must-fail.

22. Amy Vertino, "I Am an Uber Survivor," Medium, February 24, 2017, https://medium.com/@amyvertino/my-name-is-not-amy-i-am-an-uber-survivor-c6d6541e632f#.bitvjkvnd.

23. All data here come from National Science Foundation, "Women, Minorities, and Persons with Disabilities in Science and Engineering," accessed February 17, 2017, https://www.nsf.gov/statistics/2017/nsf17310.

24. Steve Henn, "When Women Stopped Coding," *Planet Money*, NPR, October 21, 2014, http://www.npr.org/sections/money/2014/10/21/357629765/when-women-stopped-coding.

25. Sylvia Ann Hewlett et al., *The Athena Factor: Reversing the Brain Drain in Science, Engineering, and Technology*, Harvard Business Review Research Report, May 2008, https://hbr.org/product/the-athena-factor-reversing-the-brain-drain-in-science-engineering-and-technology/10094-PDF-ENG.

26. Catherine Ashcraft, Brad McLain, and Elizabeth Eger, "Women in Tech: The Facts," National Center for Women & Information Technology, 2016, https://www.ncwit.org/sites/default/files/resources/ncwit_women-in-it_2016-full-report_final-web06012016.pdf.

27. Cate Huston, "The Day I Leave the Tech Industry," *Accidentally in Code: Engineering an Interesting Life* (blog), July 28, 2014, http://www.catehuston.com/blog/2014/07/28/the-day-i-leave-the-tech-industry.

28. Katherine W. Phillips, "How Diversity Makes Us Smarter," October 1, 2014, *Scientific American*, https://www.scientificamerican.com/article/how-diversity-makes-us-smarter.

29. Samuel Sommers, "On Racial Diversity and Group Decision Making: Identifying Multiple Effects of Racial Composition on Jury Deliberations," *Journal of Personal Social Psychology* 90, no. 4 (2006): 597–612, https://www.ncbi.nlm.nih.gov/pubmed/16649857.

30. Phillips, "How Diversity Makes Us Smarter."

31. Ibid.

32. Ibid.

33. Anil Dash, "There Is No Technology Industry," *Humane Tech*, August 19, 2016, https://medium.com/humane-tech/there-is-no-technology-industry-44774dfb3ed7.

34. Andrew J. Hawkins, "Can Uber Be Saved from Itself?" *Verge*, March 6, 2017, http://www.theverge.com/2017/3/6/14791080/

35. David Rock, Heidi Grant, and Jacqui Grey, "Diverse Teams Feel Less Comfortable—and That's Why They Perform Better," *Harvard Business Review*, September 22, 2016, https://hbr.org/2016/09/diverse-teams-feel-less-comfortable-and-thats-why-they-perform-better.

36. Jeff Bercovici, "Slack Is Our Company of the Year. Here's Why Everybody's Talking about It," *Inc.*, December 2015/January 2016, https://www.inc.com/magazine/201512/jeff-bercovici/slack-company-of-the-year-2015.html.

37. Tracy Lien, "'Ridiculous and Amazing' Slack Messaging App Keeps Human Users in Mind," *Los Angeles Times*, October 22, 2015, http://www.latimes.com/business/technology/la-fi-slack-butterfield-fun-20151022-story.html.

38. "Diversity and Inclusion: An Update on Our Data," *Several People Are Typing* (blog), Slack, February 3, 2016, https://slackhq.com/diversity-and-inclusion-an-update-on-our-data-7af803cedae4#.y2mdq445y.

39. Josh Constine, "Slack's Rapid Growth Slows as It Hits 1.25M Paying Work Chatters," *TechCrunch*, October 20, 2016, https://techcrunch.com/2016/10/20/slunk.

40. Ross Mayfield, "The Coming Tech Backlash" *NewCo Shift*, January 3, 2017, https://shift.newco.co/the-coming-tech-backlash-82b22e0c1198#.hclufme9b.

41. Anna Wiener, "It's Getting Harder to Believe in Silicon Valley," *Atlantic*, March 2017, https://www.theatlantic.com/magazine/archive/2017/03/the-shine-comes-off-silicon-valley/513815.

Chapter 10: Technically Dangerous

1. Lymari Morales, "Knowing Someone Gay/Lesbian Affects Views of Gay Issues," Gallup, May 29, 2009, http://www.gallup.com/poll/118931/knowing-someone-gay-lesbian-affects-views-gay-issues.aspx.

2. Ben Guarino, "Legalizing Same-Sex Marriage Was Associated with Fewer Youth Suicide Attempts, New Study Finds," *Washington Post,* February 21, 2017, https://www.washingtonpost.com/news/morning -mix/wp/2017/02/21/legalizing-same-sex-marriage-was-asso ciated-with-fewer-youth-suicide-attempts-new-study-found.

3. Mark L. Hatzenbuehler, "The Influence of State Laws on the Mental Health of Sexual Minority Youth," *JAMA Pediatrics,* February 20, 2017, http://jamanetwork.com/journals/jamapediatrics/article -abstract/2604254.

4. Mike Isaac, "How Uber Deceives Authorities Worldwide," *New York Times,* March 3, 2017, https://www.nytimes.com/2017/03/03/tech nology/uber-greyball-program-evade-authorities.html.

5. Anders Bylund, "Why Twitter, Inc. Fell 10% in February," *Motley Fool,* March 3, 2017, https://www.fool.com/investing/2017/03/03/ why-twitter-inc-fell-10-in-february.aspx.

6. Hudson Hongo, "Facebook Finally Rolls Out 'Disputed News' Tag Everyone Will Dispute," *Gizmodo,* March 3, 2017, http://gizmodo .com/facebook-finally-rolls-out-disputed-news-tag-everyone-w -1792959827.

7. Spencer Woodman, "Palantir Provides the Engine for Donald Trump's Deportation Machine," *Intercept,* March 2, 2017, https:// theintercept.com/2017/03/02/palantir-provides-the-engine-for -donald-trumps-deportation-machine.

Index

Note: Italic page numbers refer to illustrations.